M

views

from the back of the bus during W W II and beyond

by DEMPSEY J. TRAVIS

vie

from the back of the bus du

Lo. Comor.

Nav

WS

ing WW II and beyond

by DEMPSEY J. TRAVIS

DEDICATION

This book is dedicated to the late Miss Mary J. Herrick, my Civics Teacher at DuSable High School in Chicago, Illinois. She gave hope and inspiration to thousands of Negro students during her five decades in the classroom. She opened the doors of her home to colored teenage students some thirty years before the Civil Rights Movement of the 1960s. One of those students for whom she opened the door was John H. Johnson, the publishing and cosmetic tycoon.

ACKNOWLEDGEMENTS

This work would not have been possible without the patience and time of more than one hundred war veterans of World War II who willingly submitted themselves to hours of taped interviews. Their experiences were as varied as their names. The information they shared was voluminous, too much to be compiled in one book; therefore, I am going to consider "Views From The Back Of The Bus During World War II and Beyond", Volume I.

"Views. . ." could not have been translated into book form without the efforts of a team. The lead off hitter on my team was Ruby Davis, researcher and indexer. Number two at bat was Regina Wead, transcriber, computer expert and editor. She was followed by the clean-up man, Herman Cromwell Gilbert, veteran editor and writer. Next to come to the plate was the new member of the team, Curtis Hardy, artist and jacket designer.

Others who helped to make the book a reality were the following staffers from the Vivian G. Harsh Research Collection of Afro-American History and Literature: Dorothy Lyles, Library Associate; Robert Miller, Curator; Mary A. Williams, Assistant Curator; and Michael Flug, Archivist. The Harsh Collection is housed in the Carter G. Woodson Regional Library, Chicago, Illinois.

Equally important to this work is my wife who has adjusted to my peculiar sleeping and writing habits after forty-six years. She no longer complains about my junky library because now I have one that accommodates over 5,000 books comfortably.

CONTENTS

INTRODUCTION

While there have been many histories concerning the participation of Negroes in the military, including an exhaustive Defense Department study entitled "Integration in the Armed Services", none is as lucid or anecdotal as Mr. Travis' tome.

Both Mr. Travis and I were participants in the military during World War II: he as a soldier, whose activities he vividly describes, and mine as Civilian Aide to the Secretary of War. We both have memories and strong opinions.

Mr. Travis touches on the problems inherent in the inclusion of Negro troops in an institution that initially regarded them as inherently inferior and useless as members of the military establishment.

The changes in attitudes were and are dramatic, but gradual, and accompanied by some of the incidents and acts enumerated by Mr. Travis.

His views and mine are somewhat different, since, of necessity, my participation was not limited to an individual unit or the units in which Mr. Travis served.

I had the good fortune to work with men like Major General Otto Nelson, Deputy Theater Commander of the Mediterranean Theater of Operations, and Lieutenant General John C. H. Lee, Commander of S.O.S. in the European Theater of Operations. Both of these men, and others, believed that the Army was misusing a valuable military asset in the continuation of the policies of segregation that were deeply ingrained in the attitudes of those in senior positions. It is of interest to note that General Lee, who was General Eisenhower's classmate and roommate at West Point and a direct descendant of Robert E. Lee, defied all orders and opinions by instituting integration in the Forces of Europe at the time of the Battle of the Bulge. For taking this position, General Lee was relieved of his command and ended up as a Deacon of the Episcopal Church in Virginia.

It is noteworthy that the individuals and incidents referred to in Mr. Travis' book have all contributed to a military service that, while not perfect, produced General Colin Powell.

Many will learn more from Mr. Travis' lively account than from reading the rather dry historical works.

The message in this work is of extreme importance to some of the young people coming along who might be introduced to problems and attitudes completely foreign to them.

Truman K. Gibson Jr.,
Civilian Aide to the Secretary of War
Henry L. Stimson during World War II

Chicago, Illinois, April 1995

FOREWORD

By his own admission, Mr. Travis has open psychological scars on both his back and shoulders caused by the many crosses of humiliation and physical pain that he has carried silently throughout World War II and beyond. His scars have continued to fester with every full moon over a period of fifty-two years. Initially, he thought he was suffering from "psychosomatic" symptoms alone, but, when he opened up and began to talk to other "Negro" veterans of World War II, he learned that they were also having symptoms of stress that were connected to their traumatic experiences from the past. It took courage to expose his pain and the pain of his fellow veterans in this publication, but I suspect that his reward will be the restoration of self that such ventilation often brings.

In this meaningful book he notes that some veterans talked openly about the pain and degradation that was heaped upon them during the war, while others were too ashamed to discuss their Army experience even in a light vein. He has observed that some refused to talk about their pain for fear that they or members of their family might suffer some kind of retaliation from a source which was (in his opinion) supernatural. He further notes that with or without ghosts, these veterans' fears are real. In this book of individual journeys Mr. Travis recounts his personal observations of old war veterans who literally quake in their shoes at just the thought of sharing their real war experience in a taped interview. Others he has witnessed have literally cried uncontrollably and choked as they talked about the dehumanizing treatment that was visited upon them in the United States Army, Navy, and Air Force.

Many African-American World War II veterans have carried a cross of humiliation and shame to the grave, and for a non-psychiatrist this phenomena may be difficult to understand. However, to an African-American psychiatrist all of Mr. Travis' observations make sense. He has observed the fact that racism is an abuse of human rights which is identical to torture and terrorism-- a fact documented by Chester M. Pierce, M.D., a professor of psychiatry at the Harvard University School of Medicine. Torture being the deliberate, systematic infliction of physical and mental suffering, for the purpose of forcing one to submit and conform, and terrorism being the actual or threatened violence to gain attention causing people to exaggerate the strength of the terrorist group and the importance of their cause, Mr. Travis has exposed the torture and terrorism of racism that many of the black veterans experienced and which caused them to feel dehumanized and degraded.

In the effective and efficient submission-dominance system of U. S. racism, it is critical to control the perceptions of the oppressed, and for the oppressed to stay preoccupied with their overall inferiority and uselessness of their puny efforts in resisting the demands of their victimizers. Accordingly, the men who put their lives on the line for their country were bombarded with overt and covert efforts to keep them submissive. Consequently, the trauma of racism (torture/terrorism) and the trauma of war often join forces and create various trauma-related disorders which take on many different appearances such as: amne-sia, depression, dream anxiety disorder, drug and alcohol abuse, generalized anxiety disorder, panic disorder, personality changes, somatization, and post-traumatic stress disorder--the most widely recognized trauma/stress disorder which is characterized by the exposure to an extremely traumatic event which is persistently re-experienced mentally along with the persistent avoidance of stimuli associated with the event and persistent symptoms of increased arousal. Therefore, Mr. Travis' observations of the psychological scars of fear, anxiety, pain, depression, humiliation, shame, and psychosomatic symptoms would not be unexpected in many African-American war veterans.

Some African-Americans have been confused about racism and the additional circumstances of war may have heightened this confusion causing a great deal of pressure for many of the veteran's interviewed. The confusion about whether African-Americans are being tolerated or accepted by whites would be a crucial issue for African-American war veterans during the war because wars exacerbate concerns about loyalty. If you are not loyal to your country during war you are in great jeopardy, yet for an African-American it is difficult being loyal if you know that you are only being tolerated and not accepted. So many veterans may have been strained as they may have been forced, by necessity, to act as though they were loyal without ambivalence. Conversely, those African-Americans who felt that they earned acceptance from Whites during the war may have awakened to a post-war reality of only being tolerated--another stressful position. An additional bedevilment that may have been provoked by the war is the confusion of when, where, and how to fight racism and when, where, and how to let it slide. These are always difficult choices for African-Americans to make, but, during the circumstances of war and in the aftermath, such choices can be particularly crucial to survival and livelihood. Thus, we have another potential source of stress in the World War II veterans interviewed.

This text is an important contribution to the literature concerning African-American war veterans from all wars. Several theories propound that African-Americans have more pronounced effects of trauma/ stress from war. These theories note that the readjustment needs of veterans are complex, but those of African-Americans are compounded by the stresses produced by prejudice in a segregated and racist society. These theories contend that racism adds stresses to traumatic experiences such as war. Mr. Travis' work provides us with ethnographic evidence that in fact such theories are grounded in reality. Further, to do justice to African-American war veterans, the family and friends who seek to support them and the clinicians who seek to treat them for their trauma-related disorders need to understand the issue of how racism makes the war veteran's adjustment to society all the more difficult.

Dempsey J. Travis was blessed to have found some "brave ex-soldiers who were willing to talk freely without fear of being court-martialed for an imagined disloyalty fifty years after the big war." Hopefully, they too will find this book a form of validation for their experiences which will in some ways be healing for them.

Carl C. Bell, M.D.
President/CEO Community Mental Health Council
Professor of Clinical Psychiatry,
University of Illinois School of Medicine
Professor of Public Health,
University of Illinois School of Public Health

TRUMAN K. GIBSON JR. ,
Civilian Aide to Secretary of War

CHAPTER ONE

WWII FROM THE TOP
OF THE BLACK SIDE

ruman K. Gibson Jr., civilian aide to Secretary of War Henry L. Stimson, was the bridge between the War Department and the colored community during World War II. He succeeded Judge William H. Hastie, a 1930 Harvard University Law School graduate, who resigned in January 1943 because of the United States Army's reactionary policies and discriminatory practices heaped upon colored Air Corps cadets. Hastie also indicated that there were other racist reasons for his resignation, such as roping off "FOR COLOREDS ONLY" sections in post theaters; the creation of cotton curtain ghettos for Negroes on military bases; barring colored officers from the use of officers clubs; banning colored enlisted men from military service clubs and post exchanges, both in the North and the South; and, to add insult to injury, the isolation of blood plasma according to the skin pigmentation of the donor.

When Hastie resigned he expressed the hope that his assistants, Truman K. Gibson Jr., a 1935 graduate of

the University of Chicago Law School, and Louis Lauti-
er would stay so that the gains that had been made
under his shepherding could be consolidated.

Judge William H. Hastie

Although Hastie was only 36 years old, he had enjoyed a distinguished public career. He had been assistant solicitor for the Department of Interior and
Federal District Judge of the Virgin Islands (the first
Negro to be appointed to the Federal Bench). At the
time he was selected for the post of civilian aide in the
War Department, on October 25, 1940, he was Dean of
the Howard University Law School in Washington, D.C.

Being in the right place ahead of time has been Truman K. Gibson Jr.'s good fortune. When he met Hastie, he was in Washington, D.C. on behalf of Attorney Earl B. Dickerson of Chicago, making final preparation

Earl B. Dickerson
Chairman of the Board of
Supreme Life Insurance
Company of America

Charles H. Houston
Attorney and Co-counsel in
the Hansberry Housing Case.

for a team of lawyers who would present the Carl Hansberry housing discrimination case before the United States Supreme Court. The day before presenting the case to the court, Gibson's group presented it to the students at Howard University Law School, where William H. Hastie was Dean. Hastie and Gibson subsequently became fellow poker players and very close friends. When President Franklin D. Roosevelt appointed Hastie to the War Department, Hastie in turn invited young Gibson Jr. to become one of his assistants.

Next door to the Hastie and Gibson office, in the old Munitions Building in Washington D.C., was Captain Otto L. Nelson, who at that time was secretary to the Chief of Staff, General George C. Marshall. In a relatively short period of time Captain Nelson became Secretary to Henry L. Stimson, the Secretary of War, and was immediately promoted to major. Major Otto Nelson was on a fast career track, a fact that did not escape Truman K. Gibson Jr.

Truman Gibson solidified his relationship with then Major Otto Nelson by using his Chicago connections with World Heavyweight Boxing Champion Joe Louis and Julian Black, one of Louis' managers. When Joe

Joe Louis and Lou Nova in 1941.

Louis fought in the two major Army and Navy relief fights, Gibson received 50 free tickets. He in turn gave them to Major Nelson to pass out at his discretion to key individuals in the War Department. The tickets were promotion wheels for Nelson and they helped Gibson in the War Department. The wheels on Major Nelson's fast track got faster, in that he was elevated to the rank of Colonel and Executive Officer of the Joint Committee on Negro Troop Policies, which included all the assistant chiefs of staff. In Otto Nelson, Truman Gibson had made a friend for life.

Truman K. Gibson's primary tasks were monitoring, reporting, urging the effective utilization of draftees and making recommendations on how to improve the morale of the colored officers and men toiling in a "Made in America" racist environment. This was a tough assignment when you consider the mind set of the regular Army which marched to a reactionary beat that was exceptionally fashionable in the years between 1925 and 1940, a period that was corseted by keen opposition to the utilization of Negroes by the top military brass, including Chief of Staff General George C. Marshall and Secretary of War Henry L. Stimson. The Brass' greatest fears were that expanding the presence of Negroes in the military would result in demands by colored people for the nationwide right to vote and the freedom to engage in social intercourse with whites.

The utilization of colored troops in World War II was forced by provisions written into the Selective Training and Service Acts of 1940. The drafting of colored men necessitated an instant scramble to locate a place to

**Chief of Staff General George C. Marshall
and Secretary of War Henry L. Stimson**

train and house them. A quick resolution was to reactivate the shell of the World War I all-colored, 92nd and 93rd divisions. However housing them required a tremendous amount of overtime and expense to construct an infantry training center for colored enlisted men and officers in the desert at Fort Huachuca, Arizona, where the 92nd and 93rd divisons were headquartered.

Between July the 14th and 19th, 1943, Truman K. Gibson Jr. accompanied Brigadier General B.O. Davis, the first colored soldier to attain the rank of General in the history of the United States Army, on a tour of Fort Huachuca to survey racial conditions. They found that a series of incidents had occurred which had caused extreme agitation among the colored officers, and was being manifested down through the ranks of the enlisted men who served under them.

**Major General Otto L. Nelson, Deputy Theater Commander
of the Mediterranean Theater of Operations**

The segregation of colored officers in the regimental mess (dining facility) at Fort Huachuca was demoralizing. In addition, the objection by some white officers of the 92nd Infantry Division to the frequent presence of Major John A. Deveaux, a colored chaplain, and his wife in the military post restaurant put bitter icing on a stale cake. Commenting on the controversy the chaplain said: "Most white officers are too prejudiced to be fair."

The resentment and disaffection of the soldiers of color demonstrated itself in many ways. A car in which white officers of the 92nd were riding through Fry, Arizona was literally stoned by both the enlisted men and non-commission officers under the white officers' command. On another occasion a white lieutenant was severely injured by a blow to the head with a shovel while he slept in his tent during a field exercise. The assailant or assailants were never caught.

The disrespect for high ranking white officers in command of colored troops was further displayed on July 18, 1943 when a program dedicating a baseball field at Fort Huachuca was disrupted by jeers, cat calls, and boos emanating from 10,000 members of the 92nd Infantry Division. The appearance of Major General Edward M. Almond, U.S. Army Commander, on the baseball field ignited the negative reaction. Truman Gibson, turned to General Almond and said: "General, they must be booing at you because they show in hell don't know me."

A small percentage of colored enlisted men and officers demanded respect from the whites in the other Army even when the odds and racial climate indicated that favorable results would not be forthcoming. Jackie Robinson, the future baseball hero and legend, broke the mold in the Army in that he did not believe that rice was white and that pork chops were greasy. A case in point took place at the Officers Candidates School in Fort Riley, Kansas. Robinson was completing the last phase of his training when a drill officer referred to a Negro O.C.S. candidate as a stupid black son of a bitch. Jackie intervened and said: "Sir, that man is a soldier in the United States Army." The officer retorted: "Nigger that goes for you too." Wham! Jackie hit that drill master in the mouth and knocked out all of his front teeth. Before anybody could come to the officer's defense Jackie had the man on the ground preparing to do some major bodily harm.

Lt. Jackie Robinson at Fort Riley in 1943.

Joe Louis, stationed at Fort Riley at the time, got on the phone and called Truman K. Gibson Jr. in Washington, D.C. "Man! Jackie is in trouble; you better get out here right away." General B. O. Davis, Truman Gibson and Joe Louis met with the Commanding General. Joe Louis reportedly gave the general some pacifiers which included a case of Roederer Crystal Champagne and a Piaget watch. (The gifts from Joe Louis to the general saved Jackie Robinson's ass from the stockade and maybe worse.)

Jackie's reprieve was short lived in that the Army shipped him to Camp Swift, Texas where white folks had a reputation of being meaner to colored people than those in Kansas. The Mayor of the town bordering Camp Swift had earlier asked his congressman to inform President Franklin Delano Roosevelt that he would personally shoot the first nigger who came into his town. During World War II Southern bus drivers were deputized and carried side arms for the committed purpose of keeping all colored soldiers in their place at the back of the bus. Jackie, a brand new second lieutenant, was standing on the corner waiting for the bus. A bus pulled up and the driver said: "Alright nigger get on the bus." Jackie snapped: "You talking to me?" The driver recoiled: "Yes! Nigger I am talking to you." Jackie lowered his voice and said: "I think you are making a mistake. I will get on the bus when I am damn fucking ready." The driver jumped off the bus and pulled out his gun. Jackie took the gun and pistol whipped the driver.

Behind the second major confrontation, the top brass viewed Robinson as a trouble maker and thought he would be better off in civilian life. In November 1944, Jackie was transferred to the separation center at Camp Breckinridge, Kentucky where he received a honorable discharge. Truman K. Gibson Jr. said: "The Army portion of the televised *Jackie Robinson Story* as depicted in the movie was totally inaccurate."

At the time Jackie was discharged, Negro soldiers were serving in mud up to their necks in the South Pacific and snow up to their buttocks in the European

Theater. Back in Washington, in the late afternoon, the phone rang on the desk of Truman K. Gibson. On the other end of the line was now Major General Otto L. Nelson, Deputy Theater Commander of the 92nd Division, calling from Italy. The first words out of the General's mouth were: "You better get your ass over here. The failure of the 92nd at Masada and Messina is being used to finally prove Negroes can't fight."

Truman caught the first military transport going to Italy. Upon his arrival in the Mediterranean Theater of Operation, he was taken directly to General Otto Nelson's headquarters. Otto greeted Truman and gave him the following instruction: "You are going to see Lieutenant General Joseph T. McNarney. Don't be a smart ass, don't argue with him, because a report is on his desk recommending the removal of the 92nd Division."

Following a very brief discussion with General Nelson, Truman Gibson was ushered to the office of General McNarney, who expressed concern over the poor record made by the 92nd Division and particularly its failure in the Cinquale Canal area. He said he had recommendations from field commanders that the division be withdrawn from the line and placed in a quiet, defensive section. He further suggested that Truman examine a report which he had just received from General Mark Clark about the performance of the 92nd Division. The Clark Report essentially said that the combat effectiveness of the 92nd Division was not equal to that of the seven other American divisions in the theater. Truman responded with the following observations:

Secretary of War Stimson presents the Legion of Merit Award conferred by President Truman upon T. K. Gibson Jr.

• Responsibility for performance had not been spread fairly among all levels of division personnel. For instance, total responsibility for reported failures had been placed on Negro officers and men, while white regimental and battalion commanders had been praised in the report for excellent performance.

• The categorical statement of complete failure of the division was too rigidly drawn and did not include sufficient examination into contributing causes. The report placed full responsibility on the shoulders of the colored enlisted men and junior officers. It would, therefore, follow that because of their race, they could not be made into efficient soldiers and officers.

• The Army's area of responsibility was completely ignored and the reference to "individual training of the 370th" would make it appear that everything possible had been done for the 92nd Division, and yet, not withstanding, complete failure had resulted. The withdrawal of the Division from the line would be evidence for the future that Negro soldiers and officers could not be utilized in combat organizations.

General McNarney replied to T. K. Gibson Jr.'s observations with the statement that the decision with respect to the disposition of the 92nd Division would be a military one and would be arrived at after consideration of all available facts. He readily concurred in a proposal that Truman visit and submit a report on the Division, with particular reference to the influence that racial attitudes had on the performances of both enlisted men and officers in combat.

Prior to going to the Division, Truman, along with General Otto Nelson, visited Generals Clark, Truscott and Crittenberger, and discussed separately with these officers the performance record of the division. Truman and General Nelson also visited the 10th Mountain Division front and the Port area that were reportedly imperiled after the 92nd's failure in the Cinquale engagement.

After completing his visits with Generals Clark, Truscott and Crittenberger and concluding his inspection of the 92nd Division, Truman Gibson prepared and submitted two confidential reports. One report, dated March 31, 1945, was to General John Courthouse Lee, Commanding General, European Theater of Operations. The other report, dated April 23, 1945, was to John J. McCloy, Assistant Secretary of War. Both reports, while concentrating on the 92nd Division, also dealt rather extensively with the role of Negro Personnel in the Military, and on the viewpoints of some high-level commanders with respect to this role.

Looking back nearly 50 years to the time he prepared those reports, Truman Gibson recently made some revealing comments. He stated that the grandson of General Robert E. Lee, General Courthouse Lee, ironically held some of the more favorable views on military integration of any of the top commanders. Gibson further stated that General Dwight D. Eisenhower "was adamantly opposed to any integration"; therefore, instead of "individual integration" a limited form of "company integration" was permitted in the European and Mediterranean Theaters of Operation. But even this would not have been done without the active participation of General Lee. Truman Gibson also revealed that Eisenhower and Lee had been roommates at West Point, where Lee was in the top 10 of his class. Eisenhower was in the lower 200.

Listed below are some of the more significant opinions expressed by Gibson in his reports to Assistant Secretary McCloy and General Lee:

• Constant efforts have been made, and are being made, by the Supreme Command to indoctrinate every soldier with the importance of his assigned mission in achieving the final victory that now appears imminent. These efforts have paid big dividends. The racial attitudes of the men and officers throughout the Theater appear to be excellent.

**General Dwight D. Eisenhower confers
with a G. I. laborer in England.**

• Many problems will arise among service troops on demobilization since they will be among the last troops to be discharged.   Many problems that have been more or less quiescent during the period of active fighting might assume serious proportions in the absence of proper precautionary measures. The use of Negro Staff Officers in this connection, would be of great assistance to subordinate unit commanders.

• One of the most important procedural changes that will have to be made is in the method of assigning Negroes to combat units. If it is decided to retain large segregated units in the future, despite the many difficulties involved, a selective process of assignment of Negroes must be developed in order that the learning profiles in Negro and white units will be similar.

• Careful consideration should be given in future plans to the location of camps in which Negro soldiers will be trained. The fact that nearly all Negro soldiers have received their basic training in exceedingly hostile civilian communities has played a decisive role in their adjustment to the Army.

T. K. Gibson Jr. holds a press conference.

• The basic Army policy of complete segregation should be critically re-examined in light of the experiences of the 92nd Division and the results obtained with integrated combat units in the Europan Theater of Operations. . . The General Staff (should) proceed immediately with the evaluation of Army experiences, both in this country and abroad, with a view towards making appropriate recommendations with respect to future Army policies for the inclusion and utilization of Negro soldiers.

Nearly a half century after the investigation of the 92nd Division and the preparation of the reports supporting his findings, Gibson is of this opinion: "What occurred in the 92nd Division was not a complete failure of Negro officers and soldiers, but rather deficiencies of individuals and small units that resulted from many circumstances and factors. Because of this, no valid racial generalizations could be drawn, particularly since there were many Negro soldiers and officers in the division who performed well. History has proven the observations I made at the time to be correct. Although our military is not as bias free as I would like it to be, think of the rampant discrimination that would exist today if the military command fifty years ago had officially adopted the policy that colored military personnel were incapable of achieving effective combat readiness."

Today T.K. Gibson is practicing law in Chicago. He enjoys international clientele.

CAPTAIN FELIX KIRKPATRICK

CHAPTER TWO

POTHOLES BETWEEN THE WEST POINT ACADEMY AND THE TUSKEGEE INSTITUTE

F elix Kirkpatrick graduated in February 1933 from Englewood High School in Chicago, Illinois. His class was sixty percent white. The school was located in a lower middle-class ethnic community on the southwest side of the city. For reasons unknown to his parents, upon graduation Felix decided he wanted to enroll at Armour Institute of Technology (Illinois Institute of Technology) and become an electrical engineer. His singular decision to become an engineer was made in the early eve of the worst economic depression in the history of the country.

In the months just prior to Kirkpatrick's graduation, President Herbert Hoover was engaged in a desperate attempt to save his presidency and the Republican Party, striving mightily to lift the spirits of an economically depressed nation by prophesying that prosperity was just around the corner, with two chickens in every pot and a car in every garage. However, Hoover's

West Point Freshman Class of 1935

vision of a Republican motivated prosperity did not come to pass. He was defeated in the 1932 election by Franklin Delano Roosevelt, thereby ushering in a political era during which a Republican did not enter the White House as President for twenty years.

The only Negro engineer that Felix knew first hand was working as a mail clerk in the main post office. A colored engineer working as a mail clerk was not an aberration, in that a large percentage of Negro professionals—such as physicians, dentists, chemists and lawyers—worked as post office clerks, mail carriers, and Pullman Porters during the 1930s, 40s and early 50s.

Kirkpartrick and the late Neal Simeon (a vocational high school on south Vincennes bears his name) were

**Neal Simeon, fellow student of Kirkpatrick,
at Armour Institute of Technology in 1933.**

the only colored students in the 1933 freshmen class at the Armour Institute of Technology. Charles Meachum, a junior, was the only other person of color enrolled in the Instititue. Meachum encouraged Kirkpatrick to apply for an appointment to the United States Military Academy at West Point, New York because of his general scholarship and superior mathematical skills.

The first step taken by Meachum in pushing Felix's candidacy for West Point was to introduce him to Morris Lewis, the Secretary of U.S. Representative Oscar DePriest. DePriest had been elected to Congress in

**Oscar DePriest, first Negro
Congressman in the 20th Century**

1928, the first colored man to take a seat in either branch of Congress in the Twentieth Century. Lewis arranged an interview for Kirkpatrick with the Congressman. In a relatively short period following the meeting with Congressman DePriest, Felix was notified by the West Point Academy to report to the military installation at Fort Sheridan, Illinois for a physical examination. He passed the medical with flying colors.

Felix Kirkpatrick had not had an opportunity to prepare for the written portion of the examination when he received a notice from the West Point Academy advising him that the written entrance exam requirement had been waived. His short circuit admission to the Academy on the Hudson River was based on the high grade average he had maintained at the Armour Institute of Technology. At West Point the cadets called getting a waiver on the written entrance examination a "Dog Ticket".

**Cadet Felix Kirkpatrick
in the Fall of 1935.**

On July 1, 1935, fifteen days before his twentieth birthday, Felix Kirkpatrick arrived at the West Point Academy which is located in the southwest section of the State of New York, on the western bank of the Hudson River. Although the weather was hot, Felix's arrival at the Academy was draped in an odiously cold silence from both the cadets and fellow plebes.

Unlike the white plebes he was given an instant, full blown, non-person treatment. He was called "Mr. K" as opposed to "Mr. Kirkpatrick". Not one single soul spoke to him except in the line of duty. Hazing, of course, was the exception. Felix was hazed unmercifully by some of the cadets from both the Union and former Confederate states. His presence to many of them was as bitter as an over-dose of table salt in a small portion of food. There were three cadets who uncontrollably generated foam from their mouths like mad dogs in August whenever they saw him.

Several cadets assigned themselves to the task of keeping Mr. "K" on walking punishment tours in an effort to keep him from his studies. When the first grades were posted and they discovered that Felix had maintained above average grades, his tormentors were devastated because Mr. "K" had been set up to fail. The good marks caused them to pile on additional demerits for non-existing and minor infractions. His walking punishment tours were accelerated.

Walking punishment at "quick" time was the least of the dehumanizing demands on a long list of institutional racist traditions at West Point. Debasing colored plebes had been perfected into an art form between 1875 and 1936. Only four colored men in the fifty one year period had weathered the storm of racist harassment and also graduated. They were Henry O. Flipper, who graduated in 1879; John H. Alexander, who became a second lieutenant in 1887; and Charles Young, the last to graduate in the Nineteenth Century in 1889. In 1936, Benjamin O. Davis Jr. was the first colored American to graduate in the Twentieth Century.

**Henry Flipper
graduated in 1879**

**John Alexander
graduated in 1887**

**Charles Young
graduated in 1889**

In March 1936, three months before cadet B.O. Davis Jr. was to graduate, the West Point administrators were still having trouble finding nine other cadets who did not object to sharing a table with him in the dining room (Mess Hall). Kirkpatrick, who was at the "Point" for six months during B.O. Davis' senior year, never had a roommate in a barrack room for four or in a summer tent. At church he sat in a pew by himself. Felix never participated in the Wrestling Contest because he was considered untouchable. The dance coach, like the wrestling teacher, would not permit Kirkpatrick to participate while other plebes practiced dancing with each other.

At the end of his sixth month at West Point, Felix Kirkpatrick was sent home because of the excessive number of demerits that had been heaped on him by a group of cadets that had decided that one colored West Point graduate in the Twentieth Century was more than enough. Felix Kirkpatrick's grades were above average when he was drummed out of West Point; however, his thirst for education was shunted because of the cruel and inhuman treatment visited upon him at the "Point". He has never attended another university on a full time basis.

When Kirkpatrick returned to Chicago in February 1936, the popular song of the time was "Pennies from Heaven", lyrics by Johnny Burke and music by Arthur Johnston. The song was introduced by Bing Crosby in a motion picture of the same name. Felix's first job after returning to Chicago was as a porter at the L. Fish Furniture store. His wage of twenty five cents an hour was "Pennies from Heaven". During those hard times he was fortunate to get a job, period. After a short time Felix gave his portering position the unofficial title of Sanitary Engineer. The young man may have given up on higher education, but he had not lost his high self-esteem.

Kirkpatrick had worked at the furniture store only seven months when he got a job cleaning the exterior of railroad cars at the Pullman Company in the New York Central yard, the home of the famous "20th Century Limited", located at Root and Federal. His zest and attitude toward work bought him to the attention of a Negro supervisor, Howard Shaw, a graduate of Armour Institute of Technology. He promoted Felix to the position of electrician although he had had no prior experience. All the skilled workmen and common laborers at the New York Central south side yard were colored.

Felix recalls that on his second day as an electrician, the foreman asked him to go to the tool shed and get some tools to change a motor. A worker in the shed asked if he had ever changed a motor before. His reply was no. It was suggested that he go back and tell the foreman he had never changed a motor before. He followed the fellow's suggestion and the foreman promptly replied: "Well! This will be your first!"

While working at the Pullman Company, Kirkpatrick met Willa Brown, the aviatrix, at the desk of Enoch Waters. Enoch was the City Editor of the Chicago Defender Newspaper which was located at 3435 South Indiana Avenue. Ms. Brown presented herself at the newspaper office because she was seeking the Defender's assistance in recruiting candidates for the Civilian Pilot Training Program, for which she had a government contract.   Enoch suggested that Felix would make an excellent student. Kirkpatrick told Ms. Brown he was interested in learning to fly, but he had a full time job at the Pullman Company. She both explained and convinced Felix that he could learn to fly before work, after work or on weekends. Felix became an after work and weekend student at the Coffey-Brown School for three years. Initially he was put through the Screen Pilot Training Program to determine his flying aptitude before admitting him to the rigid primary and advance flying classes.

Felix was so overwhelmed with flying that he signed up to join the Air Force while going through the paces and also teaching ground school subjects at the Coffey-Brown School. He was put on the Air Force Reserve waiting list for an opening at the Negro air base at Moten Field in Tuskegee, Alabama. The white boys had a multiple of geographic choices at their finger tips, whereas the colored boys were restricted to one.

Felix received orders to report to Tuskegee, Alabama in September 1942. He was assigned to class 43-E and graduated in May 1943. The Tuskegee Airmen had all of their flight training at one base. In contrast, the white cadets had their primary training at one field, then they would go to another field for basic training, and still another for advance training. Their combat indoctrination was held at a fourth site.

All the aviation teachers at Tuskegee were colored, and the check pilot instructors were white with the exception of two. Several of the Coffey-Brown School graduates became the first instructors to train cadets at Moten Field, cadets that later became known as the legendary 99th Pursuit Squadron. The 99th was officially activated at Tuskegee, Alabama on March 22, 1941.

Picture was taken at the Harlem Airport in 1939. *(Standing fifth from left)* **is Willa Brown and kneeling** *(second from right)* **is Enoch Waters.**

After graduation, class 43-E was assigned to Self-ridge Field, where the 332nd Squadron was being formed. Selfridge was located in Mount Clemens, Michigan. The 99th Pursuit Squadron was still overseas flying combat missions when the 332nd was formed. The 99th was a basket case in that it was attached to the 79th Fighter Group, but was not considered part of the group because its members were colored.

The Air Force fights as a group, not as squadrons, so when the 99th was sent overseas, it had no support systems and had to be attached to a group, the 79th Fighter Group, as pointed out above. The only instructions that the 99th got from the 79th was, "You boys keep up". The 79th didn't want any part of the 99th. The colored squadron was considered a burden and treated like a ruptured appendix.

Col. B.O. Davis Jr. was sent back to the States to form the 332nd Fighter Group which was going overseas as a fighting unit. In preparation for overseas

Col. B. O. Davis Jr. returns to the States
to form the 332nd Fighter Group

they trained with the P-40s. Later on they shifted to P-39s; however they went overseas with P-47s.

According to Kirkpatrick, the worst aircraft that the Army or anybody could ever dream of was the P-39. Its claim to fame was that it had a 37mm cannon in the nose of the aircraft. However, when you fired the cannon the recoil made you stand still. "By the time you recovered from the canon's recoil you had lost about 30 or 40 miles," Kirkpatrick illuminated.

When the 332nd fighter group first got overseas, it was assigned a coastal patrol, which was a milk run between the Anzio Beach Head and the Island of Capri. When the 99th joined the 332nd it became a four squadron group, which was unique in that most groups had three squadrons. However, the group dispelled the myth that colored men could not fly.

Kirkpatrick left the Air Force in 1950 and became a special representative for Pabst Blue Ribbon Company in St. Louis. He was subsequently appointed Director of Veterans programs for the Department of Human Resources in Chicago from which he retired in 1987.

CAPTAIN JOHN "JACK" ROGERS

CHAPTER THREE

In A War Plane, He Did
What He Had To Do

J ohn "Jack" Rogers, was born on September 3, 1918 in Knoxville, Tennessee. Dating back to the time he was a young boy, he wanted to fly an airplane. As a kid he made model airplanes out of thin cheese-box wood, copper wire and paper. On several occasions before reaching his teens, he and one of his playmates walked beyond the city limits to the Knoxville Airport where he actually touched a plane. He did it because he wanted to be able to tell his little buddies that he had put his hands on a honest-to-goodness real airplane. Regardless of the intensity of his desire, he did not think that he would ever actually fly an airplane.

In 1939, Reletta Morgan, a young lady in Chicago, Illinois told him about a Civilian Pilot Training Program that was being organized at the Wendell Phillips High Evening School. The organizer was a beautiful, copper-colored, shapely woman named Willa Brown, an Aviatrix.

Wendell Phillips High School was located at 39th Street and Prairie Avenue.

Willa Brown *(left)* **and Cornelius Coffey in front of a plane at Harlem Airport.**

John could not believe that Willa Brown was going to teach people how to fly free of charge. When he found out that it was a fact and that the Federal Government was sponsoring the project he signed up for the course, and became a member of the first group to graduate from the Coffey-Brown Civilian Pilot Training Program at the Harlem Airport. Having received his pi-

Harlem Airport

lot's license he attempted to volunteer for the Air Force, and was told that the only position open for colored boys was truck driving. John did a quick around about face and stormed out of the recruiter's office.

In late July, 1941 the first class for colored Aviation Cadets commenced ground training with 13 students at Tuskegee Institute. John wanted to be a part of that first "Tuskegee Experiment" but to qualify he had to take a physical at the old post office building. The test was given daily, Monday through Friday. It was the aftermath of the Great Depression of the 1930s and John did not want to take a chance on losing his job as a substitute teacher with the Chicago Board of Education by absenting himself a day from work to take a physical. As luck would have it, they were giving the same exam down state in Champaign, Illinois every Saturday. John went down with several other fellows and passed the exam on the first try.

He was notified on November 9, 1941 that he had been accepted in the Army Air Corps. He traveled down to Tuskegee, Alabama on December 19, 1941 to begin his training. The train dropped him and another cadet from Detroit, Michigan off in a two horse town called Cheehaw, Alabama. The small train station was located in the middle of a wilderness that was several miles from nowhere.

When they got off the train John and the other cadet headed for the lighted section of the little train depot. An elderly white man working in the railroad station did not raise his head when John asked: "How do you get to Tuskegee?" The aged cage master did not even say "boo". John then said: "What kind of station is this that won't give a guy any information?" The old man slowly lifted his head and in a deep southern drawl retorted: "I don't want no trouble out of you boys." Like the snap of a whip, John Rogers quickly remembered he was deep in the heart of General Robert E. Lee's Confederate Country. He and his train companion hastily detoured around to the dimly lit side of the train station which was clearly marked

"FOR COLORED ONLY." They waited on the dark side of the station until the person who was delegated to meet the train picked them up.

John Rogers became a member of Class Number Five, at the time that Class Number One was still in training. The first class graduated in March, 1942. It had started with thirteen cadets, but only five completed the course and got their wings. The graduates were

John "Jack" Rogers, in one of the planes, flew as a member of the 99th Pursuit Squadron.

Captain Benjamin O. Davis Jr. of Washington, D.C.; Lemuel Rodney Curtis of Hartford, Connecticut; Charles Henry DeBow of Indianapolis, Indiana; George

Spencer Roberts of Fairmount, West Virginia; and Mac Ross of Dayton, Ohio.

John W. Rogers' mental snap shots of Tuskegee during his training period was that he was in a Jim Crow setup in a Jim Crow town. The theater had a neck high wall down the center. Negroes purchased their tickets on the left side of the ticket booth and whites bought theirs on the right side. Jim Crow practices between white and colored personnel on the Army base mirrored the town. The colored section of Tuskegee was policed by a white officer who wore loose-fitting faded overall trousers southern style. Colored military officers could not wear fire arms in town, that authority being the sole province of the white military police. Negro M.P's only authorized weapons off the post were wooden clubs.

In training they practiced Jim Crow by the numbers at Tuskegee. The primary instructors were all colored; whereas, in basic and advance training, the teachers were white. Some of John Rogers' classmates observed that some white teachers were mean spirited because it was alleged they were assigned to teach Negroes at Tuskegee as punishment. Some teachers were overt in their rabid hatred of Negroes. John W. Rogers was not concerned about attitudes; his primary objective was to successfully complete the flight training course and get his gold bars and wings. He graduated in August 1942.

The War Department, in the summer of 1942, had not made a determination on how, when or where they were going to use the Negro pilots at Tuskegee. Therefore, the "Lonely Eagles" accumulated more precombat flying hours than perhaps any other Air Corps group during World War II. Public pressure from civil rights leaders and the colored media continued to chip away at the Jim Crow mentality of the War Department in their efforts to get the 99th into action in a Theater of War.

The original 99th Fighter Squadron with John W. Rogers *(4th from right in 2nd row.)*

The War Department's dilemma gave John W. Rogers and other Negro pilots the freedom to fly around Tuskegee stacking up flying hours from August,1942 until April,1943. It was in late April that political pressure broke the dike and pushed the War Department into sending the 99th Pursuit Squadron to North Africa.

The 99th arrived in Casablanca, French Morocco on April 24, 1943. To make sure that racism maintained its proper place on the war agenda, the Army bulldozed two flying strips five miles apart, one for whites and the other for Negroes in the North Africa desert. This was designed to prevent fraternizing between colored and white airmen.

The Army realized, however, that limited fraternization could be a teaching tool. Combat was strange to all members of the 99th. Not a single pilot in the group had ever engaged in a combat mission. To alleviate this deficiency, the white brass selected Bill Campbell and Charlie Hall, two of the 99th's best pilots, to fly with a white combat group on a single mis-

Captain Charles B. Hall

sion. This, like most urban school systems for Negroes, the brass reasoned, would provide enough learning for the two selected Negro pilots to teach the other members of the 99th.

In John Rogers' opinion that capsulized combat mission was not smart.   Since there is no substitute for experience, the 99th made some mistakes.   Rogers states: "The pilots were green and their errors were blown out of proportion in the Time Magazine."   The Times' article led to a senate investigation.   Colonel Benjamin O. Davis Jr.'s testimony before a Senate

Colonel Benjamin O. Davis Jr. in a press conference following Senate Hearing.

Committee won a reprieve for the Negro pilots.   The reprieve, however, was more than warranted in that on the morning of January 27, 1944, at a time when the Tuskegee pilots were out numbered by the Germans two to one, they managed to shoot down five enemy aircrafts in four minutes, and three additional planes that afternoon.

Lt. General Benjamin O. Davis Jr. cites John Rogers in his autobiography as one of his three mainstay

John W. Rogers boards a train in North Africa shortly before the 99th Squadron went into combat in Italy.

fighters in the 99th. "Jack" recalls: "I never landed a plane if I didn't know where I was going. The first time I saw a target over enemy territory I knew and understood what I had to do. They sent a white boy over to our squadron to lead a flight. I was flying his wing. I got a certain amount of pride and I ain't going to let no white boy do more than I can do. When we reached the target he went down and I went down behind him. What you worry about is that they are shooting at him, but they might hit you. It's human to have fear, but one must remember that a coward dies a million deaths, but the brave only die once. If I have got to fight I would rather be in an airplane than anywhere else."

After John W. Rogers was discharged from the Air Corps as a Captain, he decided that he wanted to become a lawyer. He selected the University of Chicago because it enjoyed the reputation of being one of the best. He was told via telephone that he did not have the necessary prerequisites.

John was not prepared to be derailed after his successful tour as a soldier. He recalls: "I put on my uniform, with my wings and medals, and went over to the school and told them there must be some kind of test I could take to prove that I would be a good candidate for Law School."

John took the test and was admitted to the Law School. Today, as a Judge of the Circuit Court of Cook County, he sits in Juvenile Court.

CAPTAIN WILLIAM R. THOMPSON

CHAPTER FOUR

THE LITTLE COLORED BOY WHO DREAMED
HE WAS CHARLES A. LINDBERGH

illiam R. Thompson was born on January 26, 1916 in Pittsburgh, Pennsylvania. He lived in the "smokey city" until 1936, when he went away to college at Hampton Institute, in Hampton Virginia. Most of the members of his maternal family were in the medical field, in careers encompassing registered nurses, pharmacists and physicians.

Thompson's interest in learning to fly airplanes predated his teenage years. He was motivated by Charles A. Lindbergh's transatlantic solo flight to Paris, France on May 20-21, 1927. Most of the kids that he played with at Clark University Pittsburgh Lab School, in Pittsburgh, Pennsylvania were occupied with building model planes and radios. Young Bill's hunger for knowledge about aviation history and model plane blueprints stimulated him into becoming an avid reader on the subjects in both books and magazines long before he reached high school.

His interest in airplanes never waned. He enrolled and completed the Civilian Pilot Training Program

**Charles H. Lindbergh, the first pilot to fly
alone across the Atlantic Ocean.**

while at Hampton Institute where he received his Bachelor Degree in 1940 and also his pilot's license. With a degree and pilot license in hand he thought he could walk into an Army Air Corps or Navy recruiting station and be accepted without any problem.

He was wrong about his acceptablity to both the Air Corps and the Navy. Although his mother and father had not told their mulatto son that he was white, they had not stressed the fact that he was colored. Consequently, when little Bill looked into the mirror he did not see his tinged skin; he saw snow-white Lindbergh.

Bill was not the only colored person afflicted with a complexion delusion. For instance, although the author of this book has always known that he is unmistakably colored, he frequently saw himself during his pre-teen years as such movie stars as Tom Mix, the western cowboy; Tarzan, the white king of the Jungle; and Douglas Fairbank, the swashbuckling hero in such silent films as Robin Hood, Alexander Dumas' Count of Monte Cristo and The Three Musketeers.

Through a family connection, who worked in William Hastie's office in the War Department, Bill Thompson got a letter from Washington D.C. advising him to go to Cleveland, Ohio and take the C-4 Air Corps cadet examination. He passed the examination and was sent to Chanute Field in Rantoul, Illinois where he joined 400 Negroes being trained by white instructors, before being shipped down to the "Experiment" at Tuskegee Institute where an aviation program for coloreds was being established.

Out of the 400 cadets selected, six were to be trained as tactical officers, two in engineering, two in armament and weapons systems and two in communications. There were so few coloreds undergoing technical training at Chanute that separate classrooms were not feasible. Out of the six selected for special training only two are alive in 1995: Elmer D. Jones of Washington, D.C. and Bill Thompson, who migrated to Chicago, Illinois after World War II. Bill was selected to go into weapons systems and armament.

The white cadets being trained at Chanute Field were housed on the right side of the railroad tracks in high-rise brick buildings approximately one city block

First A-C Officers, Elmer D. Jones, *(front left);*
William Thompson *(front right);* **Nelson Brook
and Dudley Stephenson** *(back row).*

removed from the colored section of the field. The colored cadets lived in old wooden WWI army barracks on
the traditional wrong side of the tracks.

The white boys wore pale blue West Point type uniforms with black visor caps to class, while the colored
cadets wore dishwater green fatigues and floppy hats
of the same color and material. Bill Thompson admits
that he did not have any real sensitivity to the way
that he and other colored cadets were being treated. As
a matter of fact he found humor in such treatment.

Seeing humor in being ill-treated is not an unusual
reaction. During the 1930s and 40s colored men were
kicked in the ass by their white bosses, and had to
laugh to keep from crying in a futile effort to cover up
their humiliation. On the other hand, many white
men lost their foot while trying to kick some colored
man's behind.

After graduation at Chanute Field, Bill was immediately transferred to Tuskegee where he was assigned to Captain B.O. Davis Jr.'s flight class. However, because of his training at Chanute, he was not permitted to fly. He spent the major portion of his time watching general contractors turn muddy farm land into a mile-long concrete runway, nestling in the well of low rolling Alabama hills. The first housing surrounding the newly built runways were tents. William R. Thompson's official title in tent city was Armament officer.

After spending two years at Tuskegee, in April 1943, Bill Thompson went overseas with Colonel Benjamin O. Davis Jr. as the Armament officer of the 99th Fighter Squadron. The pilots in the squadron each had about 250 hours of flying, which was three times as much as the white boys had after going overseas and returning to the states after completing 60 combat missions. The colored pilots piled up unspecified surplus flying hours because the Army Chief of Staff could not figure out how to use colored men whom they had assumed did not have the brains or courage to fly. There was no plan in place for the 99th Fighter Squadron to see combat.

Civil Rights organizations such as the NAACP and National Urban League with the support of the Negro Press, Eleanor Roosevelt, the President's wife, and A. Phillip Randolph turned up the heat on President Franklin D. Roosevelt and the War Department to get the 99th off the runway and into the flaming skies over Europe. The prodding by the civil rights groups, Mrs. Roosevelt and the Negro media resulted in the 99th being shipped to Casablanca, French Morocco on April

24, 1943.   Bill Thompson describes the airfield in North Africa as a dry lake bed. He said that the temperature was so hot that the lake must have evaporated into the clouds.

There was no systemic indoctrination prepared for the 99th Fighter Squadron's arrival because nobody expected them to come to dinner. In fact, there was only one officer who made a real genuine effort to teach the squadron how to fly the Curtiss P-40 in actual combat. That officer was Colonel Philip G. Cochran who was the training specialist for Major Gener-

In North Africa Col. Philip Cochran (standing) **talks with Col. B.O. Davis** (inside cockpit) **as Bill Thompson leans on the plane.**

al John K. Cannon, the commander of the tactical air force in the Mediterranean Theater of Operation. Unlike the other units the 99th had been thrown in an ocean of hot sand to swim without the benefit of a single swimming lesson. Cochran became the closest thing to a life guard.

The 99th had no veterans with combat experience, in that it operated under a policy of strict racial separation that precluded the transfer into their unit any experienced combat pilots from white squadrons. Cochran's solution to the dilemma was to assign a hand full of colored pilots to the white units that were willing to accept them. His independent actions were in strict violation of the Corps' Jim Crow rules.

Another problem uncovered by Cochran was that sepia pilots had trouble navigating across the vast wasteland of North Africa. The Negroes in the "Tuskegee Experiment" had been handicapped in that they had not had any cross country flight training in the United States. Such training was prohibited because there were no "back of the bus facilities" where Negroes could eat and sleep at the various Army Air Force bases across America.

On May 28, 1943 the 99th became the orphans of the 33rd Flight Group. It was unfortunate for the Negroes because 40 percent of the flyers in the 33rd were died-in-the-wool southern whites, who treated the members the 99th Fighter Squadron like non-persons. They totally ignored them at meetings prior to combat missions. The Negroes never got any precise information during the briefing sessions; they were permitted to lap along providing they did not get under foot and cause any problems. The "red necks" called them "boys" and treated them like children.

The "boys" became men on June 2nd, 1943, when they flew their first combat mission over the island of Pantelleria in the Mediterranean Sea. Their attitude in the sky was like Joe Louis' in the boxing ring-aggressive.

One month after their first combat mission, First Lieutenant Charles B. Hall became the first colored pilot to score a verified aerial victory in World War II when he downed one enemy plane and damaged another.

Bill Thompson said: "You cannot talk about war heroes without mentioning the name of Captain John W. Rogers. He was the best diving fighter pilot in the Mediterranean Theater. I have seen Jack being briefed by the British 8th Army in reference to the Germans holding up the 8th Army's advancement in Italy. Jack carried out the British instructions to the letter. He did not care about the weather. He took his flight to the target and dropped bombs in the headquarter windows of the enemy."

Included among members of the 99th mentioned by General Benjamin O. Davis in his autobiography for indispensable service were Jack Rogers, William Thompson, Dudley Stevenson, Willie Fuller, James Wiley, Herbert Carter and Willie Ashley Jr.

In spite of heroics by colored pilots of the 99th Fighters Groups, Colonel William W. Momeyer, the Commander of the Group to which the 99th was attached, said: "It is my opinion that they are not of the fighting caliber of any squadron in this group. They have failed to display the aggressiveness and desire for combat that are necessary to a first-class fighting organization." (They said the same thing about Negroes in basketball, football, baseball and track).

Colonel Momeyer and Brigadier General Edwin J. House agreed that the "Tuskegee Experiment" had failed. Normally such a series of condemnations would have resulted in a unit's transfer or disbandment, however, the fate of the 99th Fighter Squadron had serious political, as well as factual ramifications. Therefore, the War Department placed, the "red hot potato" in the hands of its Advisory Committee on Negro Troops where it smoldered and died.

The myth that Negro men could not fly fighter planes was totally dispelled by the end of WWII in that Negro airmen destroyed or damaged 409 enemy aircraft and were awarded 95 Distinguished Flying Crosses, 14 Bronze Stars, and 8 Purple Hearts.

Bill Thompson became a teacher in the Chicago Public School system after being discharged from the Army. He retired in 1986 as a Masters Teacher.

1st LIEUTENANT GEORGE "CROW" TAYLOR

CHAPTER FIVE

The Fearless
George "Crow" Taylor

eorge A. Taylor was born in Middlesex County, Virginia on October 10, 1919. His family moved to Philadelphia, Pennsylvania in 1926 when he was six and a half years old. In 1932, during the big economic depression, the Taylors moved back to Middlesex County, where George graduated from the Middlesex County High School. Subsequently, in 1939, he enrolled in Virginia State College in Petersburg, Virginia where he studied for three years until he was notified by the Selective Service Board that he would be drafted in March 1942.

To avoid being drafted into the Army, George Taylor applied for the written and physical exams to become an Air Corps Cadet. He successfully passed them both. On December 17, 1942 he got his orders to report to the Tuskegee Institute. He traveled almost three days by train before arriving at Cheehaw, Alabama on December 20 at 1:30 a.m. The train station area was pitch black except for a single telephone pole with a dim light and an attached telephone. Taylor lifted the receiver off the phone and someone from Tuskegee answered and said they would be out to pick him and another cadet up in 30 minutes.

Taylor learned on his first day at Tuskegee that the upper classmen had instituted a class system and gave identical names to the new cadets. They were all called dummies. When an upper classmen entered the barracks the dummies had been instructed to jump to attention the same as they would for a Commissioned Officer.

New cadets in the "eternal chow line".

George was a member of class 43H. H stood for August, and for those who prayed that they would graduate in August 1943. After the cadets in class 43H finished their Ground School and basic training they be-

gan the 60 hours of flight training. The Pilot Training
Air Corps Officers were white and the Civilian Pilot
Training Personnel were all Negroes. The most famous
among the colored civilian trainers were Charles "Chief"
Anderson and Daniel "Chappie" James Jr.   James

**Daniel "Chappie" James, the first Negro
pilot to become a Four Star General.**

went on to distinguish himself in the Korean conflict,
becoming the first Negro Four Star General in the Air
Corps and the Commander-in-Chief of the North American Air Defense. James did not have to take primary
training because he taught the subject; therefore, he
went directly from civilian status to basic training as a
cadet in class 43G, which enabled him to graduate in
July 1943 a month ahead of George Taylor.

When Taylor graduated in August he was given a
two week furlough. He went back to Philadelphia to
visit his family and the guys he used to hang out with

at the Philadelphia Tribune, a Negro owned weekly. The fellows were all surprised to see him with wings on his chest and brass bars on his shoulders because 80% of the guys from Philadelphia, "the city of brotherly love," who had gone down to Tuskegee as cadets had washed out. George had kept his going to Tuskegee a secret because he did not want to take a chance of being laughed at and known as a "try to be pilot."

Army nurses of the Tuskegee Army Flying School Post Hospital.

His best buddy, Claude Dickens, was so out done with George for not telling him he was going down to Tuskegee that he blurted in his face: "I don't know anybody as black as you flying in the air except a black crow." To this day George is known as "Crow" Taylor in Philadelphia.

George "Crow" Taylor

When he returned from furlough he was given a 10 hour training lesson flying a P-40 fighter. After completing the training he was assigned to the 332nd Fighter Group. Class 43H did not have any extra air time to fly around like the members of the 99th and others who graduated in 1942. On December 20, 1943 Class 43H found themselves enroute to a port of embarkation, destination unknown. Instrument Training, Gunnery Training and Formation Training had all been jammed into one barracks bag. They were rushed into combat with different degrees of ignorance. Some

The Lonely Eagles Air Corps cadets stand in review on the field at Tuskegee.

guys were not as ignorant as others, but all were young and cocky and raring to be strapped into a plane for take off. In spite of their ignorance, all felt that they were masters of their aircraft and that there was nothing anybody else could do that they could not do better. It was a good attitude for men whose job was to fight in the air.

Fear was something George never entertained. His group used to do all kinds of crazy things, like rat racing, trying to get on each other's tail, and stalling out. Taylor had confidence that no enemy plane could get him if he saw it in time. The enemy might trap him by out numbering him but, one on one, he never had any fear that he could not take care of himself.

The first overseas opportunity that the men from class 43H in the 332nd got to prove that they could take care of themselves and others was in Naples, Italy. They replaced a white group that was flying harbor patrol, protecting convoys of ships carrying soldiers and supplies enroute to the Anzio Beach Head. They also were given varied assignments in supporting Army ground forces. They bombed bridges and sprayed tanks so the Army could advance into enemy territory.

On a later assignment they became an appendage to the 15th Air Force. The task was to support the U.S. bombers against German fighters. It was their job to see that the bombers reached such targets as factories, refineries, bridges, marching troops, and anything else that would disable the enemy.

In all cases, Colonel B. O. Davis Jr. kept the 332nd Fighter Group true to its mission. They could not break formation in attempts to become Aces because they saw a bunch of German fighters overhead. Their sole responsibility was to protect the bombers. Following that strategy they never lost a single bomber, a record that has not been matched by any other unit with a comparable length of service.

George A. Taylor flew 240 hours of combat missions before he was discharged from the service. Prior to retirement from his civilian occupation as an engineer for the Metropolitan Sanitary District in Chicago, he supervised the Deep Tunnel Project.

1st LIEUTENANT ROBERT MARTIN *(on left)*
and his brother, ENSIGN HENRY MARTIN

CHAPTER SIX

HE ROLLED OUT OF A BURNING P-51 PLANE
OVER ENEMY TERRITORY

Robert Martin was born in Dubuque, Iowa, a small city that was almost one hundred percent lily white. In 1942, there were 40,000 whites and 39 Negroes living in that tiny mid-West municipality. From 1st grade through the 12th grade he was the only person of color in his class. As a matter of fact, the city was so white that in 1990 the Mayor and the City Council placed several ads in major metropolitan newspapers inviting Negro families to come and live in "beautiful Dubuque."

The ratio of colored students at Iowa State College in Ames mirrored Dubuque in that Martin was the only student of the dark persuasion in his classroom during the entire four years he was at the school. However, Dr. George Washington Carver, the lone Negro graduate in the Iowa State College class of 1893, had gone on to become one of the world's foremost scientists in the first half of the Twentieth Century by revolutionizing the use of the peanut and sweet potato.

Dr. Carver is credited with literally saving Southern agriculture.

When Robert Martin graduated from college in June 1942 he was ripe as a peach for the Army. He was so ripe that a member of the local draft board called him via telephone and said: "Martin, if you don't report to this draft board within the next twenty-four hours we are going to send the F.B.I out there to get you." He was needed to fill the colored quota for September 1942.

On the other hand, Martin had a legitimate excuse for not immediately submitting himself for the draft in that he had applied for the Army Air Corps at Tuskegee and successfully passed both the written and physical examinations. He had been accepted, but not called. His explanation was not good enough for the all-white draft board because they had never heard of President Booker T. Washington, of Tuskegee Institute or President Franklin D. Roosevelt's Tuskegee Experiment for colored pilots.

In spite of Martin's protest, the local draft board sucked him in on September 24, 1942 and shipped him off to Fort Dodge, Iowa which was located just a little north of Des Moines. After settling in at the Fort Dodge, Martin regurgitated his Air Corps story again. This time the Commanding Officer believed that there might be an ounce of truth in Martin's tale. Therefore he verified it with the War Department and was advised by special order to hold Martin in the Reception Center until further notice.

Martin was made a member of the permanent personnel at the Reception Center. His only assignment was to work with the Supply Sergeant and pass out sheets to the thousands of recruits who came through Fort Dodge.

The local military establishment was so busy processing men and material that they did not have time to think about or practice Jim Crow. Moreover, it would have been counter productive to isolate three colored men in a fifty bed barrack.

After six months of counting sheets at Fort Dodge, Martin was finally called to duty as a cadet to be trained as a fighter pilot at the Tuskegee Air Corps in eastern Alabama, near Montgomery. After he completed his training, he became a member of the 100th Fighter Squadron. In the meantime, the 99th Fighter Squadron was fighting in a hot war in the European Theater as an attachment to the 12th Air Force, which was flying tactical support for ground troops.

When the 100th Fighter Squadron went over seas in February 1944 it was part of the newly formed 332nd Fighter Group. The group was composed of three all-Negro squadrons: the 100th, 301st and 302nd. The group was later joined by the veteran 99th, the Alpha Squadron. The new coalition of squadrons became attached to the 15th Air Force which was a support for strategic operations. Their assignments were to escort bombers to sites where they would blow up enemy oil fields, railroads, ships and factories, etc. Having four squadrons as opposed to the ordinary three worked to the advantage of those bombers that were being protected by the 332nd Group. The Germans were less likely to attack a fighter group of four squadrons as opposed to one composed of three. Moreover, despite the fact that every pilot wanted to be an Ace, Colonel B. O. Davis Jr., Commander of the 332nd, was opposed to his pilots trying to become heroes at the cost of losing a single bomber.

The white flyers from other groups would frequently get sucked into playing Ace in the sky against the German Luftwaffe. The German pilots would taunt the American flyers by making aggressive moves and some white pilots would take off, with visions of the movie hero John Wayne in mind, to play cowboy in the sky. As soon as that gap in bomber security had been broken by the wayward pilots trying to become heroes, another group of German planes would nose dive through the clouds and blow the unprotected bomber out of the sky. The Germans rarely attacked the 332nd because they stayed together as a group dedicated to the single mission of protecting the bombers. The group established an excellent reputation because they stuck with their assignment and therefore did not lose a single bomber.

When a pilot had flown five escort bomber missions he was automatically awarded an Air Medal. The medal was sent home to his parents. On the other hand, if he was shot down and no one knew what happened to him, his parents would not receive a medal but a letter stating that their son was missing in action. Missing in action was not uncommon among pilots who went on strafing missions.

Martin was on his 64th strafing mission when his plane was shot down near Zagreb, Yugoslavia in 1945. He describes the event as follows:

"Queen Cole" Martin's plane.

"After being hit, the engine began to smooth out, running quieter than ordinary. A few seconds later I noticed short tongues of flames coming from the exhaust stacks. The flames grew longer, but the engine continued to run smoothly. I stayed at tree top level for perhaps a minute to get out of sight of ground observers, and the thought flashed through my mind that I would have to bail out. The flames coming from the exhaust stacks were very colorful and in the shape of long tubes, like the balloons you see at sideshows that get twisted into animals. The tubes of flames grew longer and longer and in seconds were encircling the bubble canopy over the cockpit.

"The decision was made--you bail out or sit and become a fried charcoal Negro. I climbed to about 1000 feet above the terrain, looked out, and said to myself 'this is not high enough.' I climbed up another 1000 feet.

"To bail out, you had to disconnect the radio, oxygen, and jettison the canopy. (Some moments earlier I had sent out a 'Mayday' call saying I was bailing out). I then rolled the plane on its back, unhooked the safety belt, and thought I was dropping free and clear. I was wrong!

"I was falling out when the plane rolled over about three quarters of the way. I was falling like someone trying to run with his coattail caught in a closed door. The 300 mph wind factor was holding me attached to the plane. My body was out but my legs were still in. What to do? No debate-DO IT RIGHT. I grabbed the edge of the cockpit, pulled myself back in, sat down, grabbed the controls, leveled the plane, did a proper half roll, let go, and I was free and clear, except the tail of the plane was falling in my direction. It missed.

"I counted to ten, but wait! I was the World's Greatest Fighter Pilot. This was my 64th mission, nothing could ever happen to me. I had worn my parachute straps loose so they wouldn't bind and hurt or cut off circulation during the five hour mission. However, if a chute with loose straps was opened, the force of the leg straps catching one's crotch and genitals could cause severe damage and I would be singing soprano for the rest of my life. Now, in desperation, I wound, yes, wound my legs together like a twisted rope. I pulled the rip cord, remembering to wrap my arms around my body so I could save the rip cord to present for proof to get into the 'Caterpillar Club', the

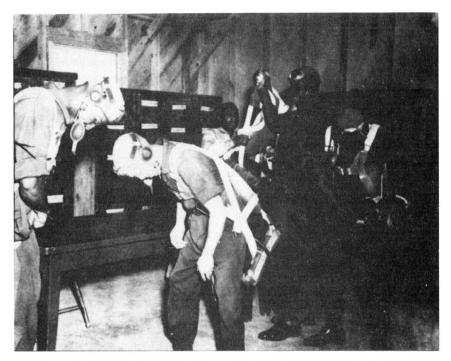

Pilots preparing for take off by strapping on parachutes.

club of flyers whose lives were saved by a parachute made from the silk thread of a caterpillar cocoon.

"For several seconds I was knocked out cold because when I came to, I was floating, and swinging down with a huge white parachute canopy overhead. In front of my face was the chest buckle, almost forming a new pair of goggles. I could taste blood from where the buckle had hit my chin, knocked me out cold and split my lip on the inside.

"I was okay, coming down over a section of woods but with an open field nearby. Instructions, 'If you pull on the shroud lines on one side, the parachute will move you in that direction.' Those are the wrong instructions. 'Your rate of descent will increase like you don't have a parachute.' It scared me to the point I'd take a chance going into a tree and I let go of the lines. I missed the woods and landed about fifty feet away. Luckily there was little wind and Î had no trouble collapsing the chute, rolling it into a ball and stuffing it under a bush. I lit out running south, away from the Germans. At mid-afternoon the sun was west of south," Martin concluded.

Since Martin had been strafing North he ran hard for about twenty-five minutes South until he came to a field that had a herd of cows. The presence of the cows indicated he was not in German territory because soldiers would have eaten them up. He laid down on the ground near a fence trying to get his breath and looking around to see if anybody was watching him. After regaining his composure, he walked across the field to a small farm house. He found a middle-aged woman and a boy about 12 years old. The lady spoke enough English to ask him if he was hungry. He nodded his head and she cooked him two eggs and gave him some grappa (wine). It was Martin's good fortune that these people were part of a partisan group fighting on the side of the Allies.

Martin spent the next month eating and sleeping in a secret Yugoslavian camp high in the mountains with the partisan soldiers. When the DC-3 Transport finally came they arranged to fly him back to Italy where he joined his squadron and was then sent back to the United States.

Martin, who is now 76 years old, lives in Chicago following his retirement as an engineer for both the Park District and the City of Chicago.

"As a fighter pilot, you fight a war on your own," Martin said. "The only way you survive is by telling yourself every day: 'I am the very best there is'."

1st LIEUTENANT HENRY P. HERVEY

CHAPTER SEVEN

ONLY THREE OUT OF FIVE
WOULD FLY

enry P. Hervey was introduced to the sky by Willa Brown, a flight instructor at the Coffey School of Aeronautics. The school was located on the southwest of Chicago at the Harlem Airport. The Coffey-Brown School was unique in that in 1939 it was the only privately owned colored institution in America with a Federal Government contract to operate a Civilian Pilot Training Program. There were six colored colleges and universities that also had the program. They were Delaware State, Howard, Hampton, West Virginia State, Tuskegee and North Carolina Agricultural and Technical.

After finishing Part I of the program, Hervey and his classmates were advised to go downtown to the old post office building and take the exam for Part II of the Civilian Pilot Training Program, which was actually the Air Corps exam. Fourteen members of Hervey's class took the exam and they all passed. They were then sworn into the Air Corps Reserve, which voided their chances of being drafted under the Selective Service Act of 1940.

After being sworn into the reserves, in March 1943 Henry P. Hervey went directly down to Moten Field in Tuskegee, Alabama. Book wise everything went smoothly for Henry and the other boys from Chicago. Their problem was classroom body language. Their

Cadets on the Tuskegee campus.

bodies were saying things that they should not be saying to white folks who generally had a very low opinion of colored people and particularly uppity Negroes from the North.

Cadet Farley, Hervey's roommate from the sovereign state of Georgia, told him he was going to teach him how to handle himself in a manner that was acceptable to Southern whites. For example, he said, "If an instructor says something that you don't agree with, you cannot say; 'you got to be kidding'. They don't want a colored cadet talking to a white officer in a manner that might even imply disrespect."

On the other hand, Farley said, "if the instructor calls you a black son of a bitch, don't take offense because if you object and ask for a court martial you are going to lose anyway. Keep in mind that the experimental Air Corps Program at Tuskegee dictates that the instructor can only pass 3 out of 5 cadets; therefore, if you have the wrong attitude you're going to be the first one to be washed out."

Moten Field did not have the facilities for training pilots to fly the B-25, which was a medium size bomber. Therefore, when Hervey completed the nine month training program at Tuskegee and was commissioned a Second Lieutenant, he was transferred along with some other graduates, to Maple Field, California. The Post Commander at Maple Field had not been forewarned that a bunch of colored officers were coming. Hence, without a script he greeted the Negroes with the following statement: "Fellas, as far as I am concerned you are members of this class of 800. Follow the rules and do the best you can. Good Luck."

The commander's remarks in 1944, signaled both a sign post and historic day in military history. Colored men and white men could go anywhere they wanted to together, bunk together, eat together and enjoy each other's general comradery. The environment of freedom lasted for approximately three weeks when a di-

A group of cadets, including Henry Hervey (standing
3rd from the left) **pose in front of a B-25.**

rective came up from the headquarters of the training
command in Texas, saying: "Pursuant to regulation
zero you are hereby directed to provide separate sleeping quarters for the colored officers on this date before
0900."

The colored officers promptly moved all of their be-
longings into a special barrack "designated for colored".
Their meals were to be served at separate tables in the
Officers Club and they were to fly in separate colored
squadrons. The flying classes were separate, in that a
certain number of planes and instructors were set
aside for colored officers. They were back to square
one with the exception that the ground classes were in-
tergrated.

Many of the colored officers decided that they were not going to be downsized by eating their meals at a special table in the Officers Club. In as much as they had to pay for their own meals out of their pocket, they opted to eat in dignity at a table of their choice in a restaurant on the base.

After about six weeks of flying lessons the base was closed down because of a heavy daily dose of rain. A decision was made to move the entire unit out to Arizona. The colored pilots helped ferry all of the ships down to the sunshine state. After white pilots were ensconced in the warmth of the state, the colored fellows were told to go back to Maple Field and do the best they could.

The best they could do was to fly at night. The rain usually stopped about 5 or 6 pm, and that's when what the Air Command thought were going to be dodo birds took to the air. They learned to fly in formation in the dark. They mastered flying by instruments in the dark. In spite of the handicaps they managed to finish on schedule and graduate with the sunshine boys in Arizona.

After the war Hervey became manager of Federal Savings and Loans and subsequently helped organize, and found Independence Bank where he later became President. He is currently an Investment Officer at Chicago Metropolitan Assurance Company.

SERGEANT LLOYD G. WHEELER

CHAPTER EIGHT

THE INCORRIGIBLE
NEGRO RECRUIT

I n the Spring of 1942 Lloyd Garrison Wheeler was recruited by the Civil Service Commission to become a civilian teacher trainee for ground personnel in the Army Air Corps. The Army Air Corps base at Chanute Field in Rantoul, Illinois was the site of the training program. At the time Wheeler was recruited, he was not aware that the teaching assignment would be a part of the Air Corps' Negro Experiment at Tuskegee.

Wheeler was a 1932 University of Illinois graduate with a bachelor's degree in Actuarial Science. He was the assistant corporate secretary at Supreme Liberty Life Insurance Company, headquartered in Chicago, Illinois, when he signed on for the job at Chanute Field. The salary at Chanute was less than what he was making at the insurance company. However, on the other hand, he was not married and there was a strong possibility that he might be exempted from military service because of the patriotic nature of the new job.

There were more than 100 other college trained Negroes recruited from across the country for the trainee
program. Each trainee was permitted to select a single
specialty from a half dozen disciplines, including, for
example, electronics, engines, propellers and frames.
Wheeler selected engines. He was impressed with the

**Recruits work on engine as part
of their training program.**

wide range of learning opportunities that studying airplane motors offered. There were three empty giant
hangers at Chanute set aside for the Ground Personnel
Training Program. In lieu of airplanes, there were row
after row after row of every kind of mechanical device
that one could wish for in a training program of this
nature.

The teachers put the trainees through a rigorous six month training program, a program that was as good, if not better, than any college could offer. The Negro instructor trainees were trained side by side with white instructor trainees. However, Wheeler soon noticed that every morning a long train of approximately 30 coaches loaded with white soldiers would pull into the air base. These soldiers, he discovered, were going thru a 10 day abbreviated ground personnel training course. The absence of Negroes among these soldiers was significant to Wheeler. He felt that Negro soldiers should be given the same educational exposure as whites.

It was the results of this and other acts of overt and covert racism that caused the 100 plus Negro instructor trainees to organize an Instructors Association to confront the military on various racial issues. Balm Leavell, the co-founder with Joseph Jefferson of the Negro Labor Relations League in Chicago, was elected President of the group, and Lloyd G. Wheeler was elected Secretary. Leavell was an aggressive, articulate, creative organizer, in addition to being hypersensitive to anything that had the slightest odor of racism.

The racial issues on the front burner were the preferential treatment given to the white trainee instructors and the discussion about building a club on the base that would exclude Negroes. These were the kind of problems that Balm Leavell could chew up and spit out before breakfast. Balm Leavell was so aggressive that some of the Negroes felt he was stepping too far over the line. Particularly, when he advocated marching on the General's office, the other Negro trainees had to pull his string.

Balm Leavell

Lester Granger

The hottest issue arose when the Negro instructors discovered that their job assignment would be restricted to the "Tuskegee Experiment". All the instructors supported Balm in his agitations against accepting a "Jim Crow" assignment. Letters over Lloyd Wheeler's signature were sent to President Franklin D. Roosevelt; Secretary of War Henry L. Stimson; Walter White, Executive Secretary of the NAACP; Truman K. Gibson Jr., Civilian Aide to The Secretary of War; Lester Granger, Executive Director of the National Urban League; and the Civil Service Commission.

In the well of Wheeler's subconsciousness the thought kept seeping through that each letter he signed was an autograph of a left wing liberal in the eyes of the military establishment. He also knew that he was being labeled a trouble maker, a tag that he would have to wear in the future.

Since the Instructor Association members were all civilians they had the right to reject any specific assignment three times without losing their civil service status. Twice they rejected any notion of accepting the Tuskegee assignment. Their objective was to expand, not restrict the opportunities for Negroes.

Maj. Gen. Walter R. Weaver delivers the Inaugural Address opening the new Air Corps School for training Negro aviators at Tuskegee.

When Wheeler's class finished the six month course, the white instructor trainees were sent to air bases all over the country; whereas the colored group stayed at Chanute for several months. The military establishment had not decided what to do with them, since they had all rejected going to Tuskegee. Wheeler's opinion at the time was that the Tuskegee ground training equipment would have to be fourth rate, when compared with Chanute Field. On a personal level, Wheeler had high regards for Tuskegee as an educational institution. His father had taught there in 1910 under Booker T. Washington, following graduation from the University of Illinois.

Frederick Patterson, President of Tuskegee

While the group was waiting to see what was going to happen to them, they did some practice teaching at Chanute. When the orders came down, the Negro group was splashed all over the country. Wheeler along with several others were sent to Amarillo Army Air Field, Texas where they taught for several months.

Negro soldiers were not allowed to use the air base service club. The Army Air Force personnel stated that their presence "would prevent the local white girls from entering the club."

The colored instructors were told by the local folks who worked at the Air Force base that Amarillo, Texas was very prejudiced and that if a Negro male entered a store in town, he better take his hat off. Wheeler tested it. However, in the author's opinion it was not a real test because Wheeler is fair skinned, blue eyed, with stringy hair. Among whites on a cloudy day he could easily pass for a white, suntanned Texan.

The real color test came on a day when Wheeler's car was in the shop. He was determined that he was not going to ride Jim Crow on a bus. He found a colored fellow with a cab who drove him to the base. At the end of the day, after he had finished teaching, he could not find a cab. Wheeler had no options except to put on his courage cap and get on the bus, which he did. He took a seat directly behind the driver. Before the driver made his next stop, he said in a gentle tone: "Would you mind taking a seat in the back before the bus gets crowded?" Wheeler ignored him and kept looking out the window. The bus driver drove on to the next stop, and in a louder tone said, "Would you mind please takin' a seat at the back of the bus?" Wheeler looked around as if he did not know the driver was talking to him. The driver repeated his request in a loud harsh tone. Wheeler recoiled: "Yes! I would mind." He then jumped off the bus, knowing that he had no means for getting back to Amarillo, except to walk 15 miles.

Wheeler had hiked about two miles when an old truck pulled up beside him and stopped. The driver threw the door open. Wheeler got in with his heart in his mouth, thinking maybe he was on the way to a lynching party. After explaining to the driver, who was an old white man, why he was walking, the driver said:

"Are you one of them niggra instructors that teach over there at the air base? They tell me all you niggra boys got a degree." Wheeler replied: "That's right." The old man retorted: "I got some kids teaching over there and they ain't got no college degree. Me and my children were born and raised in Crescent City where no niggra is able to stay after dark." It was two hours after sunset when the old truck hobbled into Amarillo, Texas.

After two months in Amarillo, Wheeler received orders to report to the Induction Center in Lincoln, Nebraska, where he was inducted into the Army. Being in the Ground Personnel Training Program hadn't kept him out after all. From Lincoln he was shipped to Fort Leavenworth, Kansas. He recalls being very depressed when he had to put his civilian clothes in a bag and send them back to Chicago.

Wheeler scored very high on the Army General Classification Test. For anybody else that would have indicated that he would be an excellent candidate for Officers Candidate School. His aggressive conduct at Chanute had put a ceiling on his Army career. The highest rank he would achieve in the Army would be buck sergeant.

Wheeler made several brief camp stops between Leavenworth and Las Vegas, Nevada. It was at Las Vegas

Army Air Base where he was ordered to park his car and get in line with some other Negro soldiers. The Negro soldiers were ordered to drop their pants down to their ankles in the middle of the street at 8:00 o'clock in the morning as soldiers and civilians were streaming by enroute to work on the base. The partially naked men were closely inspected from their ankles to their upper thighs. They were spared the short arm inspection. Wheeler was livid and humiliated.

After it was all over he told the other soldiers that he was going down to the orderly room to "see what this matter was all about." All the men said they were with him. When he reached the orderly room all of the others had dropped out. Wheeler was not able to get any immediate information about why he had been mistreated.

After a long lapse of time, Wheeler found out that a Negro soldier had been accused of raping a white girl who had inflicted a deep scratch on his right thigh. The boy that was accused of the rape was a handsome dumb Georgia boy. The woman actually had not been raped because she secretly had been going with the boy for some period of time. However, on this particular night, someone must have seen them together and she hollered rape.

Lloyd Garrison Wheeler, who feels that the Army raped him for three plus years, subsequently became President of Supreme Liberty Life Insurance some years after World War II. His memories and thoughts about his Army experience are among the things he would like to forget.

1st LIEUTENANT JAMES B. WILLIAMS

CHAPTER NINE

101 AIR FORCE OFFICERS WERE ARRESTED
FOR REFUSING TO BE JIM CROWED

J ames B. Williams was born in El Paso, Texas on May 28, 1919. His father, Jasper Williams, initially was a school teacher, but later became a homesteader. His mother, Clara B. Williams, was also a school teacher. She graduated from Prairie View Normal and Industrial College in 1905 with a teacher certificate and subsequently taught there for nine years. She later did undergraduate college work at New Mexico Agricultural and Mechanical College where she was permitted to sit in an isolated corner at the back of the room. Mrs. Williams was the first Negro to receive a baccalaureate from that college. She graduated in 1937 at the age of 51. Mrs. Clara B.Williams, the matriarch of the Williams family, died Sunday, July 3, 1994 at the age of 108. She was the "wind under the wings" of her three sons: Charles, Jasper and James, all doctors and founders of the Williams Medical Clinic on the south side of Chicago, Illinois.

James Williams attended the Washington High School for Colored in Las Cruces, New Mexico. It was a typical one room, one teacher, no library, no running water, out house school.   During his Freshmen and Sophomore years he worked after school picking cotton, washing cars and shining shoes.   When he became a Junior he got a job at a filling station, greasing cars and doing some mechanical work, which he learned on the job.

After graduating from high school he went to Wiley College for two years, New Mexico University for one year and New Mexico State for a year. Although he did not have a degree, he was offered and accepted a job as Principal at Clovis High School in Provost, New Mexico.

Williams remembers vividly that when he walked into the office of the Superintendent of the Provost School, the Superintendent was busy talking to another white gentleman.   When he looked around and saw Williams, without breaking the cadence of his conversation, he said: "That boy is going to be the Principal of my nigger school."   Williams started to walk out, but economic reasons dictated that he stay.   The Clovis High School was of the same post-Civil War vintage as the one that Williams had attended in Las Cruces.

While he was teaching at Clovis High the federal government opened a course in Airplane Mechanics and Sheet Metal in the white section of town.   Since the town of Provost pulled in the sidewalks at sunset and there was absolutely nothing to do, Williams enrolled in an Airplane Mechanic course.   He was the only colored in the class.   He completed the Airplane and Engine course requirements but did not take the exam for licensing. At the end of the public school term he went back home to Las Cruces and applied to enter the Air Corps at Tuskegee, Alabama. While waiting for a response he was drafted and sent to El Paso, Texas and then shipped to Camp Picket, Virginia where he was selected to go to the Medical & Administrative Officers Candidate School.

Williams was not interested in becoming a M & A Officer, therefore, he asked for a leave to go home. However, instead of going home, he went to Washington, D.C. hoping he could talk to someone at the Pentagon. Luck was on his side in that he met a Major in the procurement office of the Air Corps who was willing to listen to his story. As the Major had promised, Williams was transferred to the Air Corps in exactly three weeks after his visit to the Pentagon.

Special orders came through and Williams was sent to Boca Raton, Florida for three months of basic training. Following that he was sent to Yale University for six months of training in the engineering school. Twelve thousand cadets were trained in that group. Only 30 were colored. Of the 30, 28 graduated and became commissioned officers. Of the 28, eight earned Ph.D degrees after the war and two became M.Ds. All the activities at Yale were integrated, except housing.

After Yale, Williams was sent to a half dozen airplane engine plants around the country for hands-on training before being shipped to Tuskegee, where he stayed for two months while a staff for the 477 Bomber Group was being assembled.

After the 477 Bombardment Group was fully staffed, it was transferred from Tuskegee to Selfridge Field,

Cadet James B. Williams, *(1st row, 2nd from right)* **with Yale classmates.**

outside Detroit, Michigan. The stay at Selfridge was short-lived because of dissension among blacks over their inability to use the officers club. The Negro officers were pressing for equal access and the white officers took an over-my-dead-body posture. To calm the waters the military establishment moved the 477th to Godman Field, Kentucky. The move further lowered the morale of the colored officers. The white officers at Godman were permitted to use the officers club at Fort Knox, which was near the front door of Godman while Negroes were restricted to the inferior facility at Godman Field. Before the bell could ring for the contestants to come out for a second round it was discovered that Godman Field's runways were not suitable for

Lt. Williams *(on the left)* **at Tuskegee.**

bomber use.   When First Lieutenant James B. Williams and some of his fellow officers went over to Fort Knox to eat in the small Jim Crow cafe set aside for colored, through the partially open door of the officers club they could see German prisoners of war enjoying the freedom that they were being denied.

To make a bad matter worse, the bomber group was moved to Freeman Field in Southern Indiana near the town of Seymour, which was reputed to be the home of the Klu Klux Klan. Seymour was a dangerous place for a Negro to be caught after sun down. The hatred of Negroes by local whites was thick enough to cut with a knife.

Equal but separate facilities were thought by the High Command at Freeman to be the solution to the officers club problem. Negro officers protested that piecemeal Jim Crow was not acceptable. The Military Command at Freeman, the First Air Corps Command at Mitchell and the High Command in Washington were whirling like a merry-go-round with the problem when the Negro Press stepped into the center of the controversy, followed closely by the NAACP and the Urban League. The high profile news worthiness of the Freeman Field incident heightened because over 100 colored officers, who symbolized our best and brightest, were involved.

The Freeman Incident reached the boiling point when Colonel Robert R. Selway Jr. posted a notice on the bulletin board which essentially said the following: "Negroes could not use facility 123 which was the white officers club, 124 which was the swimming pool, and 235, the tennis court."

The Colonel had also denied the families of Negro officers housing, although there were a number of empty buildings on officers row. He further impotized colored officers by withholding the power to Command. Command meant having authority over white junior officers, and that was a situation the military was not prepared to accept. No Negro officer could occupy a rank that would put him above a white officer. Negro officers with combat experiences in the European Theater were more frequently made junior to white officers with no combat experience.

On April 9, 1945 1st Lt. James B. Williams was called before a panel of nine officers, eight white and one colored. The Negro officer's name was Nick Roberts. He had attended Chicago's New Wendell Phillips

**Col. Robert R. Selway Jr.,
Commanding Officer of Freeman Field**

High School in 1935 and 1936 with the author. We were childhood neighbors and fellow morning newspaper delivery boys. Chairing the meeting was Captain Tyson, a friend of First Lieutenant Williams. Captain Tyson asked Williams if he had read the petition that was posted on the bulletin board. Williams indicated that he had read the document but would not sign it.

Williams further stated: "If I don't have the same rights as you as an officer then I should not be one." Tyson bristled and replied: "I am giving you a direct order to sign. If you refuse you are under arrest in your quarters." Williams was the third officer to be ar-

1st Lieutenant Nick Roberts

rested and he was followed by 98 other Negro officers. On April 13, 1945, 101 Negro officers were lined up like convicts and flown back to Godman Field on a DC-3. Their actions in attempting to exercise their civil rights was interpreted as a violation of the 69th article of war. The document listing all of the officers under arrest read as follows:

HEADQUARTERS
FREEMAN FIELD
Seymour, Indiana

13 April 1945

SUBJECT: Disciplinary Action

TO: All Concerned

1. Pursuant to authority conferred by the 69th Article of War, the following named commissioned and flight officers are ordered into arrest in transit from Freeman Field, Seymour, Indiana to Godman Field, Kentucky, and arrest in quarters upon arrival at Godman Field until further notice, effective 0800 hours 13 April 1945:

NAME	RANK	SERIAL NO.	SIGNATURE
Arthur L. Ward	1st Lt.	0584177	————
Donald D. Harris	2nd Lt.	02075544	————
James B. Williams	1st Lt.	0867664	————
Paul L. White	F/O	T-136700	————
David A. Smith	2nd Lt.	0585809	————
Charles E. Wilson	F/O	T-62507	————
William C. Perkins	2nd Lt.	01051725	————
John E. Wilson	F/O	T-136703	————
James Whyte, Jr.	2nd Lt.	0339096	————
Paul W. Scott	F/O	T-136685	————
Stephen Hotesse	2nd Lt.	02075599	————
McCray Jenkins	F/O	T-136661	————
Werdell A. Polk	2nd Lt.	0713064	————
Harris H. Robnett	F/O	T-64629	————
Robert E. Lee	2nd Lt.	02075548	————
Donald A. Hawkins	F/O	T-67154	————
George H. Kydd	2nd Lt.	0828043	————
Glen W. Pulliam	F/O	T-66410	————
Eugene L. Woodson	F/O	T-136705	————
Frank B. Sanders	2nd Lt.	02080926	————
Charles E. Darnell	2nd Lt.	0824324	————
Walter M. Miller	F/O	T-141234	————
James V. Kennedy	2nd Lt.	0841271	————
Denny C. Jefferson	F/O	T-136714	————
Glen L. Head	2nd Lt.	02069201	————
James H. Sheperd	F/O	T-64630	————
Harry R. Dickenson	F/O	T-140092	————
Edward R. Lunda	F/O	T-140111	————
Quentin P. Smith	2nd Lt.	0841269	————

LIST (continued)

NAME	RANK	SERIAL NO.	SIGNATURE
James P. Jones	2nd Lt.	02075601	_____
Charles J. Dorkins	2nd Lt.	0841269	_____
Sidney H. Marzette	F/O	T-140114	_____
Maurice J. Jackson, Jr.	F/O	T-140105	_____
Leonard A. Altemus	2nd Lt.	02082572	_____
Herdon M. Cummings	2nd Lt.	0841277	_____
Howard Storey	F/O	T-136601	_____
Mitchel L. Higginbothan	2nd Lt.	0841164	_____
James C. Warren	F./O	T-131958	_____
Alfred U. McKenzie	F/O	T-68765	_____
Cleophus W. Valentine	2nd Lt.	0841276	_____
Herbert J. Schwing	2nd Lt.	0841273	_____
Ario Dixione	F/O	T-140132	_____
Wendell G. Freeland	F/O	T-141200	_____
Robert B. Johnson	2nd Lt.	02068898	_____
David J. Murphy Jr.	F/O	T-66406	_____
Calvin Smith	F/O	T-136687	_____
Clavin T. Warrick	2nd Lt.	0841278	_____
Lewis C. Hubbard, Jr.	F/O	T-136660	_____
Robert S. Payton, Jr.	2nd Lt.	01174673	_____
William J. Curtis	F/O	T-68763	_____
Theodore O. Mason	2nd Lt.	0838167	_____
Cyril P. Dyer	2nd Lt.	02080886	_____
Adolphus Lewis Jr.	F/O	T-140136	_____
Victor L. Ranson	2nd Lt.	02080924	_____
Luther L. Oliver	2nd Lt.	0841272	_____
Lloyd W. Godfrey	F/O	T-138243	_____
Edward E. Tillmon	2nd Lt.	02080937	_____
Coleman A. Young	2nd Lt.	01297128	_____
Frank V. Pivalo	F/O	T-136681	_____
LeRoy F. Gillead	2nd Lt.	0713060	_____
Leonard E. Williams	2nd Lt.	01054447	_____
Connie Nappier, Jr.	F/O	T-138250	_____
Norman A. Holmes	F/O	T-141212	_____
Argonne F. Harden	2nd Lt.	0841270	_____
Roy M. Chappell	2nd Lt.	02068895	_____
Robert L. Hunter	2nd Lt.	02082649	_____
Leroy A. Battle	2nd Lt.	02075525	_____
James W. Brown, Jr.	2nd Lt.	0838186	_____
Charles E. Malone	F/O	T-138247	_____
Walter R. Ray	2nd Lt.	02068902	_____
Edward W. Woodward	2nd Lt.	02882639	_____
Charles R. Taylor	F/O	T-136723	_____
John R. Perkins, Jr.	F/O	T-64270	_____

LIST (continued)

NAME	RANK	SERIAL NO.	SIGNATURE
Roger Pines	2nd Lt.	02068901	————
Alvin B. Steele	F/O	T-140140	————
Roland A. Webber	F/O	T-136696	————
Hiram E. Little	2nd Lt.	T-140137	————
Samuel Colbert	F/O	02082500	————
George W. Prioleau, Jr.	F/O	0713065	————
Rudolph A. Berthoud	F/O	02082576	————
Marcel Clyne	2nd Lt.	T-131952	————
Clifford C. Jarrett	2nd Lt.	02075547	————
Arthur O. Fisher	2nd Lt.	02060946	————
Marcus E. Clarkson	F/O	T-138615	————
Charles E. Jones	F/O	T-140108	————
LeRoy H. Freeman	2nd Lt.	02080947	————
Charles S. Goldsby	F/O	T-68764	————
George H. O. Martin	2nd Lt.	02068900	————
Wendell T. Stokes	F/O	T-140123	————
Melvin M. Nelson	2nd Lt.	02082653	————
William W. Bowie, Jr.	2nd Lt.	02080867	————
Edward W. Watkins	2nd Lt.	0814209	————
Bertram W. Pitts	F/O	T-140119	————
Edward R. Tabbanor	F/O	T-131956	————
Silas M. Jenkins	2nd Lt.	0838166	————
Clarence C. Conway	F/O	T-141193	————
Harry S. Lum	F/O	T-141228	————
Frederick H. Samuels	F/O	T-66149	————
Robert T. McDaniel	F/O	T-140697	————
Edward V. Hipps, Jr.	2nd Lt.	02068897	————
Haydel J. White	F/O	T-68712	————

2. It is ordered that each commissioned and flight officer acknowledge receipt of this order, by placing his signature opposite his respective name.

ROBERT R. SELWAY, JR.,
Colonel, Air Corps,
Commanding.

Between April 10 and April 20, 1945, communications flowed continuously between Freeman, Mitchell Field and Washington. Also during this time communication between the NAACP and Urban League were sent to Congress, Truman Gibson (Civilian Aide on Negro Affairs to Secretary Stimson), Secretary of War Stimson and President Roosevelt. The McCloy Committee also entered the picture and, following its final decision, published a report that was very distasteful to the military. Basically, the military was upset because McCloy would not undercut the decisions made concerning the officers club incidents at Selfridge, and added some recommendation to clarify the usage of facilities.

The bottom line to the whole affair was that only the three Negro officers accused of forcing their way into the club were put on trial. Because lieutenants Shirley R. Clinton and Marsden A. Thompson were base personnel they were found innocent. The third, Roger C. Terry, was found guilty of pushing past the Provost Marshal and was fined $150. In May of 1945 all white officers in the 477th were replaced by Negroes.

Following his discharge from the service on September 22, 1945 Williams entered the Creighton University School of Medicine, graduating with a M.D. in 1951. Dr. Williams did his residency in surgery at Creighton Group of Hospitals from 1952 to 1956. Upon completing his residency he was awarded a Master of Science in Surgery from the Creighton University School of Medicine. He became licensed to practice in Illinois in 1957. He is also licensed to practice in Iowa, Nebraska and Indiana.

In 1960 the three brothers, Drs. Jasper F., Charles L. and James B. Williams, opened the Williams Clinic on the southeast side of Chicago.

In addition to seeing patients at the clinic, Dr. Williams has staff appointments at Provident Hospital, St. Bernard Hospital and St. Catherines Hospital in East Chicago, Indiana. He is also the Senior Surgery Attendant at Mercy Hospital and Medical Center, Doctor's Hospital and Jackson Park Hospital.

SEAMAN FIRST CLASS DAVID C. COLEMAN

CHAPTER TEN

The Sailor
Who Wouldn't Cook

avid C. Coleman Jr., on July 27, 1945, shortly after graduating from high school at age 17 in Albuquerque, New Mexico, volunteered to join the Navy. His father, a minister of a very small church, could not afford to pay the tuition to send his son to college. David's remedy, with the blessings of his father, was to join the Navy and receive the educational benefits offered by the G.I. Bill of Rights which had been passed by Congress in 1944. Coleman was determined to accept nothing less than a seaman's rating when he joined the Navy.

Prior to 1945, a seaman's rating and an eventual petty officer's stripe seemed like the ultimate in advancement to a colored volunteer, who in the past had been restricted to serve only as a mess mate, steward, or cook.

The past was the present for David Coleman because when he was being processed through the induction center at Santa Fe, New Mexico, the white examiner felt his arms and said: "This boy is going to make the Navy a good cook." David's immediate response was: "My dad told me that if I could not go into the Navy as a seaman, not to go." He was accepted by the Navy as a seaman.

Mess attendants on the USS Wisconsin.

David Coleman was shipped to a camp in San Diego, California. He was assigned to a platoon and barrack that was all white. Shortly after he got settled in, a group of white recruits came into the barrack and one of them looked at David and said: "Hey, there's a nigger in this barrack. Don't you see that jet black nigger? Oh, I ain't going to sleep in a barrack with a coon." They subsequently started telling nigger jokes and laughing the "Mulligan Stew" out of their heads.

David was alone, young, scared, and shaking. The First Platoon leader recognized his plight and had him swapped into the second platoon which was housed on the second story of the same barracks. The fellows in the second platoon were guys from California, Oregon, and the state of Washington. They welcomed David and treated him nicely and more or less protected him against the "confederates" in the First Platoon.

David Coleman, *(Left on front row)* **at the San Diego Naval base.**

David had been the state middle weight boxing champion of the New Mexico high schools. After several weeks in the Navy he got a chance to use his ring skills to get some of the frustration out of his system. He got an opportunity to box one of the first platoon sailors who had a confederate flag tattooed on his right arm. When he knocked out the Southern white the Northern white boys of the Second Platoon cheered their brains out.

After completing boot camp in San Diego, California, David was shipped to the disbursing/store keepers school at Great Lakes, Illinois. His next stop after completing the course was Camp Oak, California. It was a recreation base for officers and therefore heavily populated with Steward Mates to serve them.

The second day at Camp Oak, Chief King, the officer in charge, told him he was being assigned to kitchen duty. Coleman said: "Sir! I am not a Steward Mate, I am a disburser/store keeper." Officer King's face turned beet red and he yelled: "Are you telling me that you are not going to follow orders. You are not going to do what I tell you to do?"

"No! sir," Coleman replied. "I just thought you may not know that I am classified as a disbursing/store keeper."

The officer, with his steel blue eyes, looked through Coleman as if he was a window and said: "I am restricting you to this base and charging you with insubordination. On Monday you are going down to see the captain."

Shortly after daybreak Monday the shore patrol came to Coleman's barrack and marched him down to the brig where he was incarcerated. Coleman was in jail for 3 weeks before he was brought before the Captain. The Captain asked him what he had done and Coleman told him. The Captain looked up from the report he was reading and said: "I could put you behind bars for insubordination; however, because you are young and have never been in trouble I am going to send you back to Chief King with the understanding that you are going to do what he tells you."

Nine Negro sailors were commissioned from the ranks by the U.S. Navy in 1944.

Coleman went back and King assigned him to the kitchen washing dishes.   An older steward said to Coleman: "I told you to keep your big mouth shut. You see what it got you."

David washed dishes for several weeks and then out of a clear blue sky Chief King sent for him to come to his office. When David Coleman entered King's office he saluted. King returned the salute and said: "I am transferring you from the kitchen to shore patrol duty." He also moved him out of the all colored barrack to an all white one because he did not want Coleman contaminating the minds of the colored stewards. Coleman, in a short period of time had got a reputation as the little colored guy who had the audacity to speak to the big bad King.

The shore patrol job was leap years in pleasantry over kitchen police. They gave him a 45 to strap around his 24-inch waist and a jeep to ride around the post in while performing his duties. David was enjoying his new job when Chief King called him and advised him that he had been put on a one man order transferring him to San Clemente Islands, which is about 100 miles off the coast of California.

When David Coleman arrived at San Clemente he found that there was only one colored person on the entire island and he was a steward mate. The steward's job was to take care of the officers. All of the officers had private quarters and so did the steward mate who arranged for Coleman to have private quarters right next to his.

Coleman was assigned to a disburser/store keeper position working with a disbursing officer and helping him prepare the payrolls. He held that position until he was honorably discharged on June 29, 1946.

The recertification of the David Coleman case was traced to a white officer who had observed the treatment that Coleman was getting from Chief King. He wrote a letter to the 11th Naval District headquarters and they directed King to take Coleman out of the kitchen. The district monitored Coleman's Navy career up until the day he was separated from the service.

Seaman First Class David C. Coleman Jr. is now the Presiding Elder, South District, of the Chicago Conference of the African Methodist Episcopal Church.

ENSIGN HARVEY C. RUSSELL

CHAPTER ELEVEN

GOOD NEWS FROM THE COAST GUARD
ACADEMY THAT COULD NOT BE TOLD

Harvey C. Russell was born in Louisville, Kentucky on April 14, 1918. Both of his parents were educators. His mother was a high school teacher and his father, Harvey C. Russell Jr., was the President of West Kentucky State College. The senior Russell was a lover of jazz music in that he gave the entire Danny Williams Orchestra four year scholarships.

The Williams' band was one of Chicago's most popular dance orchestras among both the high school and college set in the late 1930s. Young Russell, who was a student at West Kentucky State, was a jazz fan to the point that he volunteered to become the band's bus driver.

After graduating from West Kentucky State, Harvey entered graduate school at the University of Indiana. As a matter of fact he was a student at the university on December 7, 1941, the day the Japanese bombed Pearl Harbor. He was instantly recruited to fill a required government quota along with five other colored graduate students for work in a local defense plant. There were whites recruited from the streets for the same jobs. Many of them had not even graduated from high school.

The job's personal bonus for Harvey, was an automatic deferment from military service. Young Harvey found the work in the machine shop both repetitive and boring. After ten months he had his fill of the repetition and decided to quit and volunteer for the Armed Services. Both the Army and Navy were so soaked in racism that he passed both of them up for a shot at the unknown in the Marines and Coast Guards, both of which were reportedly opening their doors a wee bit wider for Negroes. The Marines wanted Harvey to come down South in the Carolinas for basic training, whereas the Coast Guard basic training facility was in Manhattan Beach, New York. He chose New York and the Coast Guard, in that order.

A fact not known to Harvey was that the Coast Guard was under the umbrella of the Navy in war time. Its current racial policy mirrored those of the Navy. However, "up until 1922, all recruiting stations were authorized to recruit Negroes under the same condition as other ethnics were recruited," according to reports from the Department of Transportation. However, in June 1922, enlistment of Negroes was discouraged by consensus of the General Boards of the Navy and Coast Guards. The Negro Coast Guards, who were rated prior to 1922, were relegated to assignments where they had little or no command authority. The 1922 directives of the board were still in effect in 1942.

Coast Guard Recruits at Manhattan Beach Training Station, New York.

The rationale for the General Boards' twenty year racist policies were as follows: (a) "The enlistment of Negroes for general service would lower the high morale of Navy (and Coast Guard) personnel and reduce the efficiency of the fleet"; (b) "Negroes have lower health, educational and intelligence ratings than white men..."; (c) "the white man considers that he is of a superior race and will not admit the Negro as an equal"; (d) the white man will not accept the Negro in a position of authority over him."

When President Roosevelt put his foot down in April 1942 and made it crystal clear that Negroes would be integrated into the general ranks in the Coast Guard and Navy, Secretary of the Navy Knox announced within hours after the President had laid down his gauntlet that Negroes would be accepted in capacities other than mess men. Coast Guard Commandant Rear

Prior to the Secretary of the Navy's announcement that Negroes could serve in other capacities, mess men regularly served officers.

Admiral Russell R. Waesche had a plan ready to test whether or not integration of Negroes would be effective.

Harvey C. Russell became part of the Admiral's test when he began active service in the Coast Guards in October 1942. He was in a class of 600 and he finished 5th in the class and was appointed instructor in the School of Signaling.

The plan under which Harvey went into the Coast Guard was terminated in December 1942. For the balance of World War II, the Coast Guard came under the Selective Service Law, which involved a racial quota system. An average of 147 Negroes were inducted each month during 1943. The impact from the stream of new Negroes necessitated a revision of personnel planning. Negroes with Steward's ratings had been functioning on important battle stations whenever they were needed. Dorie Miller, the Pearl Harbor hero, was a classic example of a mess man behind a gun.

Dorie Miller, the Pearl Harbor hero.

In December 1942 Joseph Jenkins, a Civil Engineer from Detroit, Michigan, was the first Negro to be admitted to the Coast Guard Academy. He graduated in April 1943 and thereby became the first Negro to become an Ensign in either the Coast Guard or the Navy. He was assigned to the Boston District, as Executive Officer of the Constitution Base, which was made up of a 90% white crew. He held that position until he was assigned to the U.S.S. Sea Cloud.

U.S.S. Sea Cloud

High ranking officers of the U.S.S. Sea Cloud, *(Top left)* **Ensign Joseph Jenkins,** *(kneeling bottom right)* **Ensign Harvey C. Russell.**

Seaman 2nd Class Harvey C. Russell remained at Manhattan Beach as an instructor until October 1943, when he was admitted to the Coast Guard Academy. At the Academy he was treated as any other cadet. He was assigned to quarters and classes alphabetically without even a hint of animosity or discrimination. After two weeks at the Academy he was called to the office to talk to several high ranking officers, and advised not to notify the Negro newspapers or attempt to get any publicity while at the Academy. "If you flunk out they will accuse us of having done it because of race," the officers told him. Harvey followed their instructions to the letter in that he remained quieter than a mouse on Christmas Eve until he was commissioned. Harvey later learned that Jenkins had been given the same instruction about publicity. Harvey was the only Negro who went through the Academy as a Deck Officer and Jenkins was the only one who went through as an Engineering Officer. Jenkins and Russell, in fact, were the only two Negroes to graduate from the Academy during World War II.

In spite of the fairness that both Jenkins and Russell received at the Academy, the majority of the Negroes were being treated unfairly in the Boston District. Commander Perry, the Commandant of the 1st Coast Guard District, called a meeting of all the commanding officers of the Weather Patrol Fleets running out of the Boston District and asked that they cooperate in taking Negroes out to sea with them. All of them refused to accept Negroes with the exception of Captain Sweitzer of the Sea Cloud who said it made no difference to him, as long as they were good men and hard workers.

Veterans of the U.S. S. Sea Cloud *(left to right)*
Lt. Clarence Samuels, Ensigns Harvey Russell
and Joseph Jenkins.

The attitude of the Commanding Officers who refused to accept Negroes was supported by the Naval segregation polices to which the Coast Guard had to adhere because it was under the Navy's jurisdiction. A solution to the problem was proposed by Lieutenant Carlton Skinner in June 1943. He suggested that a group of Negro Seamen be provided sea-going experience in a completely integrated operation. The Commandant agreed and Lieutenant Skinner was promoted to Lieutenant Commander and assigned to the weather ship Sea Cloud as Captain. He put together an integrated crew of 173 officers and men, out of which 4 officers, and 50 petty officers were Negroes.

Although the Sea Cloud was de-commissioned in November 1944, after a year of operation, its purpose was served. It was determined that an integrated crew is like any other crew. The accomplishments of the experiment paved the way for other Negroes to commence duty on crews that were not completely segregated.

Alex Haley, the author of "Roots" and "The Autobiography of Malcolm X", served on the Sea Cloud and benefitted from the U.S. Coast Guard's experiment. When he enlisted in 1939 as a Steward's Mate, in spite of his college training at State Teachers College in Elizabeth City, North Carolina, his only function was to assist the cooks in numerous capacities including removing dishes from the table and washing them. However, before he completed his twenty years of service he had moved

Alex Haley, the author of "Roots" served on the Sea Cloud.

up the command ladder to Chief Journalist and made his final curtain call as a Coast Guardsman in the position of Assistant to the Public Relations Officers at the Coast Guard Headquarters.

THIRD CLASS PETTY OFFICER MARK E. JONES

CHAPTER TWELVE

THE NAVY WAS THE SHADOW
OF JIM CROW

Mark E. Jones Jr. was born in Indianapolis, Indiana on October 14, 1920. He graduated from the "FOR COLORED ONLY" Crispus Attucks High School, although up until 1928 all schools in Indianapolis were integrated. After high school he studied at Tuskegee Institute in eastern Alabama until his money ran out at the end of the second semester. He then spent a year at the University of Indiana in Indianapolis where he studied, hung around with the guys and worked on a part time job. His studies, work and social life gave him a full plate.

In the Spring of 1941 World War II was near the top of the American agenda. In late July of the same year the first 12 aviation cadets in the Negro experiment commenced ground training in a barracks at Tuskegee Institute. On March 7, 1942, 5 of the 12 cadets, including West Point graduate Captain B. O. Davis Jr.,received their wings at a ceremony held at the Tuskegee Army Air Force base theater. Charles DeBow, a home town boy from Indianapolis, was one of the 5 graduates.

Mark Jones read about DeBow's accomplishments in an article entitled "I Wanted Wings" in the American Magazine and decided he wanted to be an Air Force pilot. In the pursuit of accomplishing that goal he convinced four of his drinking buddies that they should join the Air Corps with him and become the Five Brown Eagles from Indianapolis. They even projected that after they got their wings they would come back to Indianapolis and buy five Red Cabs because the Red Cab companies' drivers were not accepting colored passengers in 1942.

On Monday morning following a weekend that whiskey bottles had no bottoms, the Five Brown Eagles decided to fulfill their pledge. Thus, they all went down to the Air Corps Recruiting Station to sign up. Mark Jones, Clifford Chambers, Sherman Polly, James Dickerson and Hebert Hines all flunked. One of the eagles had a heart murmur, another was too fat, and Mark was color blind. He could not tell the difference between red and green, and his other two drinking buddies were in the early stages of physical disintegration. The Five Brown Eagles never got out of the nest.

Mark still wanted to do something other than be drafted into the Army. Fleetwood Munford McCoy Jr., a friend that he had met at Idlewild, Michigan, a summer resort for colored people around the midwest, suggested that he join the Navy with him. Mark accepted his suggestion. However, before going down to the Navy recruiting station Mark managed to borrow a Navy color chart book and memorized all of the num-

bers, thereby eliminating the possibility of being rejected because of his inability to distinguish colors.

Mark completed his boot training at Camp Robert
Smalls, a Navy facility for "Colored Only" located within the greater Great Lakes Training Center, forty miles
north of Chicago. Although the Navy Department decided in early 1942 to accept coloreds for general ratings outside of the Stewards Branch, there was little, if
any, sentiment against segregation within the Navy
Bureau of Personnel.

Special segregated service schools were set up for
Negro recruits at Camp Smalls. There were schools for
cooks and bakers, gunner mates, radiomen, signalmen, yeomen, storekeepers, quartermasters and others. Mark was selected for the quartermasters school
because of the high score he made on the aptitude
test. In quartermaster school he was trained in navigation, which was a top category for enlisted men.

After finishing school Mark received a third class
petty officer's rating, but the Navy establishment had
not made a decision on how to use his talents. Equally important was the fact that his rating was for the
right arm as opposed to the left. A right arm rating
means you work above deck, whereas the left arm rating indicates that you work below deck as a cook, bak-
er, fireman, waiter or steward.

The right arm rating did not shield Mark from Jim
Crow. When he had his meals he ate them in the
mess hall reserved for coloreds. When he went to a
Navy basketball or baseball games he found that the
teams were lily white. On the other hand, Negroes

from Camp Smalls were permitted to play on the Great Lakes Football Team.

Camp Smalls was named in honor of Robert Smalls, a Negro slave and Civil War hero who piloted Confederate transport ships out of Charleston Harbor, South Carolina. In 1862, in the still of the night, he delivered a transport ship and his family to a Yankee squadron. He subsequently was given his freedom and made a pilot in the Northern Navy.

The Commander of Camp Smalls was Lieutenant Commander D. W. Armstrong, the son of General Samuel E. Armstrong, the founder of Hampton Institute, the school that was the fountain-head for such men as Booker T. Washington, the spearhead of Tuskegee Institute; Robert S. Abbott, publisher of the Chicago Defender; and John J. Sengstacke, Abbott's nephew and publisher of the Sengstacke newspaper chain.

As a third class petty officer in the Chain of Command, Mark Jones became a Company Commander (in the Army that would be equivalent to a Staff Sergeant). His duties included pushing boots, teaching them boat order drills and discipline, as well as inspecting their living quarters. The boots thought they were being trained to go to sea and see the world when, in fact, they were being prepared to pick that cotton and tote that bail as stevedores on docks somewhere in the South Pacific or the Ammunition Depot at Port Chicago in California. This was the Depot where 320 men were instantly killed at 10:18 p.m. on July 17, 1944 after being engulfed in a gigantic explosion that blew them into small scraps of human flesh.

**Robert S. Abbott, Publisher
of the Chicago Defender.**

**John H. Sengstacke, Publisher
Sengstacke newspaper chain.**

Most of the 200 Negro men who died in the blast had been trained at Camp Smalls. This disaster was clocked as the worst of that type to take place within the confines of the United States during World War II.

Joseph Small, one of the survivors of the disaster, was trained at Camp Smalls in 1943 and was shipped directly to Port Chicago, California. He states: "It was one of the largest Naval Ammunition Depots. Everybody there above petty officer was white. All of the munitions handlers were Negroes. We off-loaded ammunition from box cars and loaded it on ships." There was no school at Camp Smalls where the boots were taught ammunition handling.

Sailors in the general service move ammunition.

Following the disaster there was no counseling, teaching, or explaining to the survivors as to what caused the powerful man-made explosion.

In the absence of any explanation 328 of the surviving ammunition loaders were ordered, three weeks after the 'night of death', to go back to work loading the same powerful material. Two hundred fifty-eight of the men refused to return to work for fear that they would suffer the same fate that had been visited upon their Negro brothers.

All of those who refused were thrown into the Navy jail where they were harassed, cajoled and threatened by white Naval officers. Since the threats did not play well on the Negro brothers' mind-set, they finally singled out 50 of the men that they considered ring leaders and charged them with mutiny, court-martialed them, and sentenced them to prison terms ranging from 8 to 15 years.

In 1990, forty-six years after the Navy convicted the 50 colored sailors of mutiny, an effort was begun to exonerate them. Twenty-five members of Congress, including five Representatives from Northern California, asked the Navy Secretary Lt. Lawrence Garrett to review the case to "Ameliorate an unsavory chapter in the history of the segregated Navy" and set aside the convictions if they seemed unwarranted.

At the time of the original trial, Thurgood Marshall attended as counsel for the National Association for the Advancement of Colored People. After an unsuccessful appeal, he called the trial a reflection of the Navy's "whole vicious policy toward Negroes."

After Mark Jones was discharged from the Navy he enrolled at Roosevelt University where he received his Bachelors Degree. He subsequently received a Juris Doctor Degree from Loyola University in 1950. He entered the private practice of law before becoming a judge in the Circuit Court of Cook County, Illinois.

He retired from the bench in 1980 and re-entered the private practice of law.

CORPORAL CLEMENTINE SKINNER

CHAPTER THIRTEEN

THE WARRIORS BEHIND THE FRONT LINES WORE SKIRTS

Clementine Skinner, a tall beige beauty, was working as a clerk for the F.W. Woolworth Company on 47th and South Parkway (King Drive) in Chicago when she met Lieutenant Ruth Freeman, whose recruiting office for the Women's Army Auxiliary Corps was on the second floor of the same building. After several meetings with Lieutenant Freeman, Clementine signed up to join the WAAC.

On July 17, 1943 Ms. Skinner received a letter instructing her to go down to the Sixth General Service Area Headquarters, which was located in the Civic Opera House on North Wacker Drive, to be inducted into the WAAC. She was the only colored among 23 women inducted that day. Following the swearing in ceremony they were told to go home and wait for further orders.

When the orders were received by Skinner several weeks later, they were from the Women's Army Corps, as opposed to the demised Women Army Auxiliary Corps. Under the auxiliary a member could walk off the job without penalty whereas in the Women's Army

Corps members were part of the regular Army, received the same pay as male soldiers, and were subject to the same punishment as male counterparts for violating any of the Articles of War.

On September 3, 1943 Private Clementine Skinner traveled to Fort Des Moines, in Des Moines, Iowa by train to the same site that was used as a Colored Officers Training School in World War I. The Basic Training was integrated, but almost everything else was segregated. The colored WACs had their own Mess Hall, USO, and Service Club. Colored women could not play in the white band because of the restriction against Negroes and whites sleeping under the same roof. The colored barracks and white barracks were in different locations of the camp. The theater, post exchange, chapel and hospital morgue were integrated. Private Skinner said she did not give a lot of thought to the Jim Crow setup, except she felt it was strange.

Since the colored who were musically inclined could not play in the white band they started a pick up marching band of their own. This was a real feat since only a few potential members of the "wanna be" band had ever held a horn in their hands. Lenore Holmes Brown, an accomplished musician, decided she would start a chorus within the band. In addition, members of the all white 400th Army Forces Band gave the colored WACs private lessons on the instruments of their choice. After several months of wood shedding (practicing on instruments) they were good enough to accept invitations to play for band rallies and recruiting drives. In the summer of 1944 the colored band was invited to Chicago to play at the NAACP's Annual Convention. Dr. Charles Drew received the NAACP Spin-

The 404th army services band were comprised of recruits from the members of the Women's Army Corps.

gard Medal that year for his pioneering work in Blood Plasma Research. Private Clementine Skinner, as the band's soloist, sang "One Alone" which was introduced by Robert Halladay in the operetta "The Desert Song" (1926). The speakers on the program were Marshall Field; Walter White, the Executive Secretary of the NAACP; Daisy Lampkin, the NAACP Field Secretary; and Oscar Brown Sr., President of the Chicago branch of the NAACP.

After the convention was over the members of the band were told that they would have to disband because of budget cuts. The young ladies cried profuse-

The 404th Army Services Band Chorus in concert on July 9, 1944 in Chicago, Illinois.

ly. Clementine, however, was not the crying kind. She soberly said to the group: "We all know outstanding people across the country. Let's start a writing campaign. Our first music director is from Jacksonville, Florida and she knows Mrs. Mary McLeod Be-thune, a friend of President Roosevelt and his wife, Eleanor. We have some folks here from Baltimore who are acquainted with Daddy Grace. I know A. Phillip Randolph, Earl B. Dickerson and Milton P. Webster."

Within a week after the letter campaign began, Walter White, Lester Granger of the Urban League, and A. Phillip Randolph, organizer of the March on Washington, had a meeting with Secretary of War Stimson. The next word the girls heard was that they would not

A. Philip Randolph and Eleanor Roosevelt in 1943.

have to disband and that they would officially become the 404th Army Service Forces Band.

In November 1944 Clementine Skinner's father died and she applied for a discharge to come home and take care of her mother. It took 9 months for the request to filter up through the Army bureaucracy. She was discharged from Fort Sheridan on V.J. Day, which was August 14, 1945. Dr. Clementine Skinner retired from the Chicago Public School System as one of the assistant principals of the South Shore High School, four decades after the war.

The racial climate at Fort Des Moines, where Clementine Skinner received her Basic Training, was two shifts above neutral when compared with the experiences other colored WACs had across the country, as the following episodes indicate.

While waiting in a bus station at Elizabeth Town, Kentucky on July 19, 1945, three Negro members of the Womens Army Corps (WAC) were set upon by white civilian police. The beating occurred when they failed to move promptly when they were ordered to leave their seats in the "FOR WHITES ONLY" waiting room. They had selected to sit in the white waiting room because the "FOR COLORED" area was jammed packed like a can of sardines. One of the hill-billy, tobacco chewing cops got happy and crashed his club against the skull of one of the young women and snarled: "Down here, when we tell niggers to move, they move." Although blood was gushing out of the young lady's nose, mouth and head wound, the brute of a cop continued beating her. When the oldest member of the trio attempted to shield her, she was kicked, mauled, and dragged across the street and thrown in a jail cell.

When the three young women returned to their base at Fort Knox, Kentucky the commander told them that they would have to appear before a court martial. The court martial was dropped when it was discovered that Kentucky had no law requiring separation of races in railroad stations, bus stations and other public buildings.

In July 1943 four WACs quit the Army at Camp Breckinridge, Kentucky because they had been trained at Fort Des Moines to be Army Supply Clerks, but in Kentucky they were assigned to scrubbing floors on their knees in a warehouse and stacking beds. The final degradation came when they were ordered to wash painted walls in the laundry.

The young women were allowed to resign under the new regulation which incorporated the former WAAC into the Army as WACs. The WACs who resigned were Ruth M. Jones, daughter of the Rev. Russell C. Jeter, pastor of Tabernacle Baptist Church, Atlantic City; and Beatrice Brashear, Gladys Morton, and Viola Bessups, all from New York City. The War Department agreed that the young women had been given an improper assignment.

At Fort Deven, Masschusetts four WACs were given one year prison terms and dishonorable discharges for refusing to scrub floors and wash windows. Private Anna C. Morrison, 20, of Richmond, Kentucky, told the court that she would rather die than continue doing work in the hospital which white WACs were not required to do. The other convicted WACs were Johnnie Murphy, 21, Rankin, Pennsylvania; Alice D. Young, 23, Washington, D.C. and Mary Green, 22, of Conroe, Texas. A civilian lawyer representing the WACs said: "The differentiation made in the assignment of work resulted in a state of mind called monomania."

Neither Army rank nor monetary wealth will shield a Negro from the impact of racism. A classic example is Major Charity Adams Earley, the first colored woman in the WACs to be commissioned as an officer. The major recalls several incidents in her book <u>One Woman's Army</u>, from which I am going to paraphrase. She said that on one occasion during Officers Candidate School following a gas mask drill they were lined up to clean their individual mask with the same chemical and same cloth, when one of the white candidates re-marked that she could not use a cloth that had been used by colored girls because she had to put the mask on her face. The room got quieter than a fly spitting on cotton.

**The women with gas masks on during
a drill which led into a Gas Chamber.**

Traditions are frequently changed when a Negro unexpectedly becomes a part of the equation. In this instance First Sergeant Adams Earley should have been the first WAAC officer to be commissioned because the first two letters of her last name were AD. To avoid

Soprano Marian Anderson, with accompanist Franz Rupp, were visiting Company 8 officers *(left to right)* **Major Charity Adams Earley, Captain Jessie Ward and Captain Ruth Freeman.**

giving that honor to a colored woman, they abruptly changed from the alphabetical order of presentation, as listed on the program, to presenting the graduates by platoons, which meant that the Third Platoon, the "colored girls" brought up the end in the graduation exercise.

The members of the WACs of the 6888th Postal Directory Unit parade in Rouen, France where Joan of Arc was burned at the stake.

Colored WACs in formation and inspection line in England.

High Negro achievers will always be at the bottom of the Bell Curve in the minds of racist whites and colored right wingers.

WILLIAM COUSINS
CIRCUIT COURT JUDGE OF COOK COUNTY
FORMER 1st LIEUTENANT

CHAPTER FOURTEEN

SHAFTING BLACK OFFICERS
DURING THE KOREAN WAR

Williiam Cousins was born in Swifttown, Mississippi on October 6, 1927. His parents moved to Chicago in the 1930s. Shortly after they arrived in Chicago his dad lucked into a back breaking common laborer's job working at Wilson and Company in the stockyards. His mother got a job in South Shore working on her knees as a domestic, which she continued to do all of her working life, except for three years during World War II when she secured employment in a defense factory.

Young Cousins was the first member in his family to finish college. At DuSable High School he was an honor student and president of the senior class. He also was the recipient of a scholarship to the University of Illinois at Urbana where he completed his undergraduate work in June 1948. He was one of three Negroes in a graduating class of 500.

While at the U of I, Cousins applied to Harvard, Yale, Michigan, and Columbia law schools. He recieved invitations from all four schools. He selected Harvard. When he arrived at Harvard in Cambridge, Massachusetts in August 1948, he sought to affiliate with the National Guard in the Massachusetts Military District as an infantry officer. He had been an ROTC officer at the U of I, commissioned as a second lieutenant in the infantry reserve. There were no colored infantry officers in the Massachusetts National Guard and they were not receptive to the idea of having any; therefore, Cousins remained unattached to a military unit.

His suspended status with the Army began to change rapidly when the North Korean Army swarmed across the 38th parallel on June 25, 1950. In the fall of that year he received orders to report to the 101st Airborne division on January 2, 1951. He withdrew from Harvard Law School in early December 1950, and returned home to Chicago to make preparations to report for duty.

Prior to being called to active duty, he had requested that he be given a few months stay to finish law school, arguing that he was being penalized because of the discriminatory practices that existed in the Massachusetts Military District. He further made the case that he was being called because he was an unattached infantry officer. Had he been attached to the Massachusetts National Guard, he would not have been called unless the entire unit was called. To his surprise the order to report for duty on January 2, 1951, was rescinded and he was permitted to finish law school, providing he presented himself for service the day after graduation.

Four of several thousand
DuSable High School Graduates
Who Served In WWII

Lt. William M. Jordan

Corporal Willie R. Maxwell

Sgt. Raymond Conley

Private Albert Johnson

After graduation he traveled to Fort Devens, Massachusetts where he ran into what he considered blatant racism. Although he was an infantry officer he was assigned to the Quartermasters, which is a labor intensive corp historically restricted pirmarily to Negro troops.

Cousins immediately became an irritant to his commanding officers in that he was constantly raising the issue about being in the Quartermasters instead of the infantry. After several months of listening to the sound of Cousins' voice, the commander decided that the only way he could get him out of his ears was to ship him off to Fort Dix, New Jersey. Cousins served at the Dix installation for several months before receiving orders to report to Fort Benning, Georgia for additional infantry training prior to being shipped over seas.

Anticipating that at some point while in the Army he would be shipped South, Cousins bought a car. He purchased the car primarily to avoid the Jim Crow traveling arrangements of public transportation. His mind set was such that he did not submit easily and readily to the impositions of racial discrimination.

One night Cousins decided to drive from Fort Benning, Georgia to Montgomery, Alabama, which is a comfortable distance, to see a friend. While driving along the dark and moonless highway, he noticed a bright red light flashing through the rear window of his car.

He stopped and two Sheriff Patrolmen walked up to his car. One told him he was speeding. Cousins agreed. Then out of the blackness of the night, one of the patrolmen shouted: "Nigger, don't you see the color of my face". Cousins responded in the affirmative. The patrolman's voice got thunderously loud as he recoiled: "Well, talk like it". Cousins replied: "Yes! sir." Simply letting those words roll over his lips transmitted mental shock waves throughout his body. Then he was told to use the Uncle Tom word, "Mister", which he did, as his heart figuratively jumped through his chest.

Having humbled this proper speaking Negro, the semi-illiterate patrolman, displaying a sardonic grin that had spread across his sunburned, moon-shaped face like syrup on a pancake, barked: "Black boy, you get in your car and drive on down that road and don't look back".

On another occasion a fellow white Army officer with whom Cousins had been friendly for several months blurted out: "Bill, where did you learn to speak like that?" His reply should have been "The same place that Franklin D. Roosevelt did." A deeper meaning to the question was the resentment that Cousins had created because of his articulating abilities. His diction grated on this officer's last nerve and he was manifesting ill feelings pertaining to it.

When Cousins reached Korea, he was initially assigned as leader of a 60 millimeter mortar platoon. The infantry company commader was white and right out of the bowels of Mississippi. The First Sergeant was also white and from some place deep in the heart of Texas. Both of them were terrible people. Cousins had not been in Korea a month when he observed that both the company and battalion commanders were

**WILLIAM COUSINS
IN UNIFORM**

systematically shafting young Negro officers. The turnover of platoon leaders was fast; consequently, a Negro could become a company commander as a result of the high mortality rate on the front line. However, instead of moving colored officers up the organizational scale, they moved them out.

Moving things along in a democratic order would mean that within a decade there would be a large Negro presence in the upper ranks of the officer's corp. This possibility obviously was taken note of by white military leaders. To circumvent this eventuality they shafted young colored officers by moving them out and giving them bad reports, or putting them on dead end or excessively dangerous assignments. Cousins was a first hand witness of the unfair treatment and complained about the systematic shafting of Negro officers.

Cousins' constant complaints caused his company commander to inform him that he was being relieved as the leader of a platoon. He was reassigned, pulled off the front line and sent to the island of Chejro-do, where he was given the lowly assignment of Mess Officer.

Second Lieutenant Cousins, in his disgust, wrote letters to the Department of the Army outlining his grievances and indicatng the pattern that was being systematiclly put in place to shaft young colored offcers in

Korea. To his amazement he got direct communication with General Joe Stillwell Jr. who was stationed on the island of Koje-do. The General arranged for Cousins to fly from Chejro-do to Koje-do in a small plane to discuss the alleged conspiracy.

After hearing Cousins' story the General told him he should be promoted, and made arrangements to have Cousins transferred from the Mess Hall into a new platoon. Two months after the transfer, he was ceremoniously promoted to the rank of First Lieutenant. The company commander and the battalion commander, who had been accused of shafting Negro officers, lost their commands following an investigation that confirmed that Cousins' allegations were correct.

As part of his extensive military career, Cousins also served two years in the U. S. Army as an infantry platoon leader during the Korean War. As a graduate of the Army Command and General Staff College, he retired in 1976 from the U. S. Army Reserve Corps as Lieutenant Colonel in the Judge Advocate General's Corps. The Honorable William Cousins Jr. is currently serving as Circuit Court Judge of Cook County, Illinois.

SERGEANT DEMPSEY J. TRAVIS

CHAPTER FIFTEEN

A SOLDIER'S FACTS AND
THE WAR DEPARTMENT'S FICTION

Dempsey J. Travis was born at St. Lukes Hospital at 14th and Michigan Boulevard in Chicago, Illinois on February 25, 1920. As a very young boy he use to play soldier with the colored and white neighborhood children; however, he never thought he would be a real one. His father, Louis Travis, and uncles Otis and Joe had been soldiers in World War I, from June 10, 1917 to November 11, 1918. They often talked spiritedly about President Woodrow Wilson's contention that they had fought the war to end all wars.

President Wilson had lied, of course, because on September 9, 1942, exactly 23 years and some months later, young Travis was marching off to fight in World War II. His first stop after being sworn into the Army was the Reception Center at Fort Custer in Battle Creek, Michigan. He was lucky in that on his second day in camp he was selected out of a group of several hundred recruits by a Major Peterson, the Reception Center commander, to become a member of the per-

President Woodrow Wilson

manant personnel in the 1609th Service Unit. That arrangement was perfect because it permitted Travis to go home every weekend after he completed his eight weeks of basic training.

All good things must come to an end, and that is exactly what happened at Fort Custer in April, 1943 when Travis refused to buy a fifth of whiskey for First Sergeant Hammond out of the money he had earned playing piano at the U.S.O. dances for colored soldiers in downtown Battle Creek. Hammond retaliated against Travis by arranging to have him shipped out under special orders, without warning, on a troop

Members of the 1609th during calisthenics.

Private Dempsey J. Travis at home on his furlough, in October 1942, visiting with his mother, Mittie and his father Louis Travis.

train under armed guards to the Camp Shenango Replacement Depot in Greenwood, Pennsylvania. Camp Shenango was a holding station for troops awaiting shipment overseas.

The sealed special orders under which he was banished from Custer must have read, "Destination Hell" because that is exactly what he found at Camp Shenango. He had not realized the depth of discrimination in the military until he arrived at Shenango. There racism was naked as opposed to being draped in its Sunday best, as had been the case at Camp Custer.

From the moment he arrived in Shenango, on a cloudy rainy Wednesday morning, he was riveted with the emotion that colored people had no status, no rights, no dignity and no rightful claim to even a niggardly amount of humanity. The hellishness of Shenango was symbolized by the slimy, black, stinky mud he wadded in up to his ankles when he stepped off the train. The stench of the black Pennsylvania mud consumed him mentally, giving him a feeling of being buried alive. He realized that such a thought, if prolonged, could drive him mad.

Negroes comprised 10 percent of the soldier population at the huge military installation. Colored soldiers were camouflaged from the white soldiers as much as possible. The barracks for the Negroes were about a mile and a half from the main gate, near the edge of the woods. Their quarters were a perfect replica of the racially segregated cities that mirrored America.

Living conditions for Negroes on the military base were deplorable. They did not have use of the PX (post exchange) or any of the recreational facilities that were re-

"Those German prisoners of war wouldn't eat if I allowed you to sit near them!"

served for American whites and German prisoners of
war.

For Negroes there were no paved roads, just mud,
and no movie theaters--just huts. Negroes at Camp
Shenango were supposed to efface themselves, stay
out of the way of white folks and literally ride in back
of the bus. Pennsylvania was "the Mississippi of the
North." The German prisoners of war rode in the front
of the bus and Negroes stood or sat in the back of the
bus, if seats were available.

Army food at its best was bad. The chow served in
the colored mess hall was worse. Some parts of each
meal were not edible. Bad meat and under cooked wa-
tery "shit on a shingle" (powdered eggs) were staples at
breakfast. At every meal there was a new outrage.

One afternoon Private Travis went to the mess hall
for dinner and found soldiers jumping up and down on
the tables, and stomping the food in their trays. Since
Hammond had sentenced Travis to a living hell, he
knew that he must give serious thought about the
ways and means to retain his sanity.

Colored soldiers who needed medical attention were
suspect if they showed their faces on the "white" side
of the camp. Travis was sent to the hospital because
he had hurt his foot on an obstacle course. A white,
middle-aged doctor with a rank of full colonel, asked
him, without a smile or an examination, "Boy, what's
your problem?" Travis replied: "My right leg and foot
are in pain, Sir." "Your what?" the doctor shouted.
"My leg and foot have been hurt, Sir," Travis replied.
"Where is the blood, nigger?" the doctor asked. "The
injury is internal and didn't break the skin, Sir," was
Travis' response.

"Boy!" the doctor snarled, glaring at Travis, "a nigger's feet are supposed to hurt. Don't you show your black ass in this hospital again trying to goldbrick (avoid work) unless you're bleeding, and I don't mean a nose bleed."

To break the spell of daily humiliation some colored soldiers shot craps on doubled blankets spread out over the latrine floor where the lights were on 24 hours a day and within an arm's reach of men sitting on the toilet stool. Sometimes the gamblers would shout in chorus, "Roll those dice, baby needs a new pair of shoes," or "Daddy needs some money to make honey with Bonnie." Occasionally a kneeling crap shooter would look up at a soldier sitting on the toilet and growl, "Cut it short and mix some water with that shit."

By the seventh week Travis was at Camp Shenango, the post authorities had begun to worry about racial conflicts that might result from the infusion of the large number of colored soldiers daily being shipped into the Replacement Depot. Despite the make-shift theater, the spark that would light the flame was the colored soldiers in large numbers who were trying to gain entry to the white post exchanges and the white movie theaters.

The morning of July 11, 1943, was hot and dusty. Travis said to Norman "Kansas" Taylor, his upper bunk mate who hailed from the Sunflower state, "Let's stay in the barracks and play cards until it's time to go to the movies and see *Wuthering Heights*, featuring Laurence Olivier and Merle Oberon." A small, makeshift, totally inadequate theater had just been built, almost overnight, for colored soldiers.

"Okay," Kansas replied, "if the game is draw poker with a 5-cent limit." Kansas was in good spirits and talked non-stop about his ambitions as they played cards. He had an undergraduate degree from an Eastern college and planned to go to medical school when he got out of the Army. Kansas maintained his cheerful composure in spite of all the miseries of life at Camp Shenango. The only thing Travis ever heard him complain about was the white commanding officer who refused to select him for the Army Special Training Program, a program that would have allowed him to enter medical school while still in the Army.

The hours passed quickly that Sunday. Travis and Kansas didn't go to lunch because they heard that they were serving a dish that they jokingly called "dear old billy goat" because it was always as tough as shoe leather and tasteless. To this day, Travis believes they were being fed horse meat. At 5:30 pm they hit the chow line and then went to the small make-shift theater. The line was already too long for them to catch the first show, so they discussed going into Sharon, a small town about 20 miles away.

Kansas was against it. "Let's wait until next Saturday and go into Youngstown (Ohio) where we can ball," he said. They played blackjack while waiting for the second show to start.

When they came out of the movie, a large group of Negroes were milling around in front of the theater. They went over to see what was going on. A Negro soldier had just got both his eyes kicked out because he tried to buy a beer in the white post exchange, they were told.

"A colored soldier's been hurt" someone screamed.
"Let's go down there and get those cracker bastards!"
Kansas and Travis stared at each other, wondering
what they should do. Before they could make a decision, a caravan of Army trucks, filled with white military police carrying M-1 rifles and double-barreled
shot guns at the ready, pulled up. On signal, the
lights in the ghetto section of the post were turned out
and the MPs opened fire on unarmed colored soldiers
standing in the middle of the street. Kansas and Travis tried to break for cover, but it was too late. The
screams and cries of soldiers who had been shot
pierced the hot July night air. Travis was knocked to
the ground by a blunt force. He saw Kansas lying near
him. Travis didn't realize he had been shot until he
felt a warm, sticky substance soaking his pants leg
and his shoulder. There was more gunfire, and then
silence.

Several Army ambulances pulled up within minutes
after the shooting stopped. Medics with flashlights
stepped over the wounded who were bleeding, moaning
and screaming in the middle of the dirt road. The
medics were trying to determine who was dead, who
was alive, and who warranted a trip to the hospital or
the morgue. When they reached Kansas and Travis,
they used their flashlights to motion for stretcher-
bearers. "Can you walk?" a medic asked Travis. He
tried, but Travis was too numb to move. They turned
Travis over and one medic said to the other, "This nigger has been shot three times." Then they turned their
flashlights on Kansas. "They got this one in the stom-
ach, but he'll be all right."

What did they mean? Did they mean Kansas would be all right and Travis wouldn't? As Travis laid there preparing to die, his thoughts were not of heaven or hell. He was cursing the darkness. The blood oozing from his body was polluted with hate.

On the way to the hospital, Travis heard the ambulance driver say to the medic, "Why the hell do we shoot our own men?"

Tech 5 Dempsey J. Travis managing the Main Army Post Exchange at Aberdeen Proving Ground in Maryland.

"Who said they were men?" the medic replied. "We shoot niggers like rabbits where I come from."

At the hospital, Kansas was rolled into a small room and Travis was left on a cart in the corridor. After a few minutes, a doctor rushed into the little room where Kansas laid motionless. Through the partially opened door, Travis could see the doctor lift Kansas' eyelids. The doctor then put a stethoscope to his chest, then tried without success to straighten Kansas' bent legs. The doctor turned out the lights and closed the door. Norman "Kansas" Taylor was dead.

Ironically, Travis became the manager of the Main Post Exchange at Aberdeen Proving Ground in Maryland, exactly one year after Taylor was killed.

THE WAR DEPARTMENT'S FICTION

Despite the alterations to make life more bearable for Negro troops at former Camp Shenango, the official military position regarding the mayhem that had occurred on July 11, 1943 remained one of cover-up and justification, as indicated by the letter reproduced on the following pages. This letter, which was written less than two months after the violence occurred, did not come into Travis' possession until 40 years later, despite serious attempts on his part to secure any defining information during the intervening years.

Walter White, Secretary of the NAACP

Walter White, Secretary of the National Association for the Advancement of Colored people received the following letter on September 6, 1943:

APPENDIX A

OSA/bc 2 E 924

OCS
WD 221.1   KAR:cib   WAS/ml
(14 Jul 43) OB-C   4371

September 4, 1943.

Mr. Walter White, Secretary,
    National Association for the
        Advanceent of Colored People,
            69 Fifth Avenue,
                New York, 3, New York.

Dear Mr. White:

        This is in further reply to your letter of July 14, 1943, concerning an incident which occurred at the Shenango Personnel Replacement Depot involving colored soldiers.

        The report of investigation reveals that on the evening of July 11, 1943, an altercation arose between white and colored soldiers who were present in one of the post exchanges. This altercation expanded until it involved a large number of personnel in that section of the camp. This affray did not reach dangerous proportions, however, and was shortly brought under control by the Military Police which consisted of both white and colored soldiers.

        Later that same evening, two colored soldiers were apprehended without proper passes and placed in the guard house. Upon arrival at the guard house, they harangued the other colored prisoners with exaggerated and lurid statements of the incidents which had occurred earlier in the evening. The colored prisoners subsequently affected a prison break and when joined by other colored soldiers forcefully entered supply rooms where they secured a quantity of firearms and ammunition. In quelling this disturbance, the Military Police, which was again composed of both white and colored soldiers, killed one of the colored rioters and wounded five others.

The Shenango Replacement Depot is, as you know, used to quarter troops who are awaiting shipment overseas. The recreational facilities at the Depot are not as elaborate as those which the men enjoyed when they were undergoing training at their former posts and camps. In this connection definite steps to improve the living conditions and recreational facilities at Shenango have recently been taken.

The investigation discloses that your informant presented an exaggerated and prejudiced picture of what actually occurred and that no colored soldier was ever handcuffed to a telegraph post as reported by your informant. It is also noted that your anonymous informant failed to appear before the Board of Inquiry which was open to all persons having knowledge of the incident. Since the War Department has evidence that Axis-minded agitators are attempting to foment racial disturbances, I would suggest that the disclosure of his name as well as the names of those who supplied him with this information would assist the War Department in its efforts to eradicate the sources of such subversive activities.

The incident, and especially the death of Private Norman Taylor, who appears to have been an unwilling participant in the riotous disturbance, is indeed most regrettable. It may be of interest for you to know that Private Taylor stated before his death that he had been in his barracks and was told to come outside by a colored soldier and fight or he would be killed.

The suggestion contained in your letter for the formation of mixed units has been considered at various times by the War Department and the decision reached that such action would be inadvisable.

The War Department is doing everything within its power to promote the mutual respect and the common welfare of both white and colored soldiers. I am sure that you will agree with me the mob action is, however, not a proper or efficacious means of promoting any cause.

Your rightful interest in this matter is appreciated and I am certain that you, as a patriotic American, will use your high position to assist in the suppression of unverified rumors which serve to increase racial tension and to impede our war effort.

Yours very truly,
Secretary of War.

COPY FOR: Acting Civilian Aide to the Secretary of War.
Operations Branch, AGO _____ Ext. 2053

FIRST SERGEANT HAROLD WASHINGTON

CHAPTER SIXTEEN

AN ARMY BUCK PRIVATE WHO BECAME MAYOR OF CHICAGO

Harold Washington was born in Chicago, Illinois at the Cook County Hospital at 11:11 p.m. on April 15, 1922. His father, Roy, was a lawyer and minister, and his mother, Bertha, was an intelligent, beautiful robust woman with a leaning toward pursuing a career in the theater.

In 1937, at DuSable High School, Harold opted to join the Reserve Officers Training Corps (ROTC) in place of taking gym because he felt that he got enough exercise practicing for track meets three to five hours daily. Although Harold didn't have any thought of ever going to war, he realized the ROTC training gave him a leg up on soldiering, in that he learned close-order drill and how to use many kinds of weapons ranging from a M-1 rifle to the 105 MM Howitzer.

Harold dropped out of DuSable High School at age 17 in June of 1939 to join the Civilian Conservation Corps (CCC). Legislation establishing the CCC was pushed though Congress in 35 days after President

President Franklin D. Roosevelt

Franklin D. Roosevelt was inaugurated on March 4, 1933. Unlike most of the young men Harold had to get his father's permission to join the Corps because he was under age.   He also was from a middle class home, whereas the majority of the boys who signed up to work for a dollar a day plus three hots and a flop were from dirt poor families. Twenty five of the thirty dollars earned monthly by the young men were allotments to help their depression-stricken families.

The colored CCC boys served in segregated companies the same as their fathers had in World War I. Over 200,000 Negroes enrolled in the program between 1933 and 1942. They were all issued two dress uniforms, two work uniforms and two pairs of thick-soled tan Army shoes, plus a raincoat and a heavy weight Army brown winter coat.   The Army Engineers constructed the camps which normally consisted of four barracks. Each barrack would accommodate 40 to 50 men.   In addition there was a mess hall, a day room and officers quarters. The Army ran the camps and the U.S. Forest Service supervised the boys' daily chores which were mostly manual. The tools used to accomplish their task were shovels, sledge hammers, double edged axes and cross cut saws.

The CCC camps were run very much like the Army, minus close order drills and guns.   The boys were awakened each morning by the sound of a bugler playing reveille. They lined up smartly at reveille for roll call in the morning and again for lowering the flag during retreat at sunset. The men made the chow line on time or missed the meal. G.I. discipline governed the camps.   Every camp had a sports program which included boxing, basketball, and baseball. Red Schoendienst, an infielder with the St. Louis Cardinal baseball team, who later became a Hall of Famer, served in the CCC in Illinois. Six months of the Civilian Conservation Corps was as much as Harold could digest.

'Uncle Sam Wants You' was a popular poster.

The USS Arizona was one of the more seriously damaged United States ships at Pearl Harbor on December 7, 1941. Many of the more than 2,000 officers and enlisted men killed at Pearl were buried alive in ships like the Arizona.

Although the Germans had invaded Poland in September 1939 while Harold was still serving in the Civilian Conservation Corps, he did not envision that that action would possibly lead to him being called to arms to defend a "democracy" that was as foreign to him as "Alice in Wonderland."

Harold had not been out of the CCC camp a year before President Roosevelt signed into law the Selective Service Act, the first peace-time military draft in U.S. History. Within ten months following the attack on Pearl Harbor on December 7, 1941, the Army accelerated its call for colored soldiers when the United States joined its Western allies in the invasion of North Africa. Harold was sworn into the Army in November 1942, and shipped out of Chicago from the Illinois Central Station at 12th and Michigan Avenue to Fort Custer, Michigan, near the city of Battle Creek, where he was processed through the all colored 1609 Service Center.

Washington's stay at Fort Custer was approximately 72 hours, during which time he officially became an "old soldier" after receiving his metal dog tags, which bore the serial number 36395331, inoculation shots and a duffle bag full of Army gear. He was told that it was mandatory for soldiers to wear their dog tags at all times because this was the Army's means of determining the blood type of wounded soldiers and the identification of dead ones.

Following the short stay at Fort Custer, Michigan, Pvt. Washington, his high school friend Theodore Davis and approximately 230 other Negro recruits were shipped by train in Jim Crow cars to Tonopah, Nevada for basic training. After a couple of days at Camp Tonopah, an Army Air Force base, it became obvious to Washington and the other young soldiers that they had been shipped to the wrong camp because Tonopah had no infantry basic training facilities. The young recruits simply marked time in place for several months.

There was a soldier at Camp Tonopah with the surname of Shields who was a former Davis Cup tennis player. He asked Harold to help him recruit a boxing team to participate in the regional Golden Gloves finals, which were to be held in Reno, Nevada, about 100 miles from Camp Tonopah. Harold recruited a team of boxers in the upper six weights. Theodore 'Red' Davis, a former co-captain of the DuSable High School football team, was their heavyweight. Harold was the light heavyweight. Another guy whose name Harold could not recall was the middleweight. They trained hurriedly for about about three weeks. It was tough because the camp was approximately 6,000 feet above sea level, and none of the fellows were accustomed to exercising in that thin air.

Dawn finally broke after what seemed like an extremely long night of anticipation to Harold and his boxing team members. That was the day they were to make the trip to Reno, the gambling capital of America. They were told that they would be staying at the Hotel Golden. Harold never forgot their arrival at the hotel; they went in through the back door. They didn't stay in a hotel room, but in a converted pantry or storage room where seven cots had been set up. Hotel food supplies had been stacked into a corner of the same room. The colored soldiers had been moved around to the rear of the hotel so fast they didn't know

what was going on. For Harold and his boxing team-
mates this was a very humiliating experience. During
the five days that they were there, they occasionally
sneaked out the front door, which was the "FOR
WHITES ONLY" entrance. What kind of way was that
to treat American soldiers in uniform who were prepared to bleed to the very end for their country? Harold asked himself.

One day Red said, "Let's get out of this windowless
pantry and go to Harrah's Gambling Casino." Harold
wasn't much of a gambler. He played a little poker,
but he wasn't going to play that kind of stuff out there.
Anyway, they went to Harrah's and Red gambled a little bit. As Harold recalls, a fellow walked up to them
as they were standing there watching a roulette wheel.
He said, "No colored allowed."

Harold said, "What?" He really didn't understand
him at first. The floor man repeated, "No colored allowed." Then Red said, "What did you say?"

So Harold and Red made a game out of it. And the
floor man finally, in disgust, walked away. After that
encounter, to make a long story short, they walked
around in the casino with a sort of a braggadocio strut
for about 10 minutes and then split. It wasn't Harold's
first encounter with prejudice; however, the racial
wound was deeper because it was his first encounter
with blatant racism as a soldier. Harold remembers
after he got back to the pantry in the hotel, he was
pretty upset about it. He wanted to get the hell out of
town. But Shields calmed them down. They went on
and fought in the tournaments. Red got beat pretty
bad in his bouts. Harold lost one of his three bouts.

Max Baer, the former heavyweight champion of the world, was the referee. Harold believed he would have had a better chance if Baer had not been the referee. Red obviously had gone along for the trip because he wasn't really a boxer.

Two days after they returned to Tonopah from Reno, they were shipped to Hammerfield, California, which was a training ground. They stayed there for approximately 13 weeks, after which Harold went to March Field, California where he stayed for several months. While there, he went to every damn school he could think of. He attended the Chemical Warfare School and Administration School, which came in handy later because he was subsequently made a First Sergeant. He enrolled in something else that you would never think or imagine, a Soil Technician School, which he described as a fascinating business. The other school that he attended was the Camouflage School.

The Soil Technician School taught him how to test soil, clay and gravel to determine whether or not the ground would support an airfield. When he came out of Soil Technician School at March Field, he was made a Staff Sergeant, the one with "T" in the middle of three stripes up and one stripe down.

On May 13, 1944 the battalion received its sailing orders. Amid the blare of the military band, and the friendly Red Cross workers passing out hot coffee and donuts, a lot of tearful soldiers boarded the U.S.S. Grant for destination unknown.

The worst conditions that one could imagine about the troop ship U.S.S. Grant would, if voiced, be an understatement. The quarters were closet-like, dirty and depressing. The food was ill-prepared, unappetizing in appearance and the taste was no better. If it was the

Staff Sergeant Harold Washington

intent of the cook to make the men sick, he succeeded. The rocking motion of the ship caused many of the soldiers to suffer miserable bouts of sea sickness.

Blackouts on the U.S.S. Grant were a nightly occurrence that scared the living hell out of the men who thought a Japanese air raid was imminent. The shrill peals of the practice alerts in total blackness did not make them feel any easier. Apprehension was ever present, even when the soldiers were gambling, watching a movie, or playing a friendly game of bridge below deck.

Rumors of land being sighted on the seventh day at sea were thick as flies over an open garbage can. Then, on the morning of May 22, Diamond Head, the famous cliff-like structure at the entrance of Honolulu Harbor, loomed ahead. The land-starved soldiers hung over the rails of the ship like hungry dogs, eagerly anticipating their first look at a topless Hawaiian female wearing a skimpy grass skirt like those worn by Dorothy Lamour in her many South Sea Islands movies with Bing Crosby and Bob Hope.

The men were really disappointed when they did not see a single girl when they debarked, and they were immediately directed to board an open train. The destination was a tent city in Kahuku, at the end of an airstrip runway and out of sight of the white folks. In addition to mosquitoes, the tents were skimmed day and night by B-24 bombers taking off for points west. The battalion had not been on the island a month when it suffered a tragedy. One of the oldest and, in many of the men's opinion, the most conscientious non-commissioned officer was reported missing. The

Tent city in Kahuka, Hawaii.

The clothes of Staff Sgt Ryan J. Coleman, "A" Company supply sergeant, were found on the sands of the Princess Beach. His body was never recovered.

On July 15, the battalion moved to Hickam Field, which the Japanese had rendered impotent during the Pearl Harbor sneak attack on Dec. 7, 1941. There the supplies were checked and superfluous material was discarded. The trucks, jeeps and other vehicles were greased, painted and conditioned for the anticipated adverse terrain and weather conditions. Three land ship transports (LSTs) were assigned to the unit, and loading them was their immediate task at hand.

On August 6, the battalion boarded the ship and on August 8 they sailed. Rumors had the boat going every where from Sakhalin to Singapore. There were about 50 ships in the convoy, consisting mainly of LSTs, with mine sweepers and destroyer escorts playing a protective role. Secrecy necessitated a zigzag route, but the general direction was south by west toward the Solomon Islands.

The ships were much smaller than the U.S.S. Grant, but living conditions were 100 percent better. Some men occupied bunks below, others had improvised shelters on deck. One large tarpaulin and several smaller ones were used to shelter the deck dwellers from the weather. Others lived under trucks that had been anchored to the deck. For diversion, there was gambling, but Staff Sergeant Harold Washington's time was consumed with reading. Books were handled gingerly and passed on; one particularly popular novel, Sanctuary, made a complete cycle of every reader on LST 737.

There were numerous submarine alerts throughout the voyage. Frequent practice in aircraft defense and nightly blackouts reminded the men that the game that they were playing was a deadly one. The deficiency of the salt-free water made rationing a necessity. Clothes were washed by the unorthodox method of tying them to a rope and trailing the apparel in the sea, letting friction do the work. There were occasional storms, but the nights on the Pacific were indescribably beautiful.

On September 12, the men were assembled on the deck of the ship and given debarking orders. The task force was to bombard and invade the islands of Pelelieu and Angaur, in the Palau Group, which were situated at the western extremity of the Caroline Islands.

The 1st Marine Division was to invade Pelelieu on the 15th. The 81st Infantry Division, of which Staff Sergeant Harold Washington was a part, moved in on Anguar, the pear-shaped island which was one mile wide and two miles long, and densely forested. The Island's defenses were not enumerated. It was expected that the men would encounter a formidable force. And they did.

An invasion of the Philippine Islands was in the making, and the Division was to help pave the road for the invasion by building a bomber strip on Angaur, jointly with the 1884th Engineer Aviation Battalion. The convoy arrived at its destination on the night of September 14, 1944. Aerial and naval bombardments started the next day.

On September 19, the task force's survey party began construction of the center line of the runway. Dock detail fell to Company "C", and September 23 saw most of the men landed and part of their equipment unloaded, although a choppy sea created a hazardous blanket of water over the pontoon bridges. Bulldozers pulled equipment over the unstable beach.

A dense jungle growth, about 500 yards from the proposed runway, was cleared for the battalion area. Foxholes, command post and SU offices were immediately set up. Snipers, mosquitoes, humidity and heat, and the steady rumble of artillery made the night one long damnable hell. Everyone wanted a medic to sleep in or near his foxhole. Mingled with the wet smell of the forest was the tangible stench of dead bodies.

By October 15, the battalion that included Harold Washington and the 1884th Engineer Aviation Battalion had made the runway serviceable but by no means complete. A C-46 and C-47 landed on the 17th of that month and the first bomber rolled the length of the strip four days later. For getting the runway in service in an incredibly short time of 20 days, the 1887th and the 1884th engineering aviation battalions received the Meritorious Service Unit Award.

Although only half the Japanese on the island were accounted for, the island was declared secured September 20. Those Japanese who remained were bottled up in caves and gorges on the northwestern portion of the island. The infiltration, sniping and food pilferage were a constant worry and danger.

Meritorius Service Unit Award

On September 31, several men were seriously wounded by gunfire. Sgt. Wilbur Rice and Pvt. Bruce Dunn died in a hospital that night.

Sgt. Wilbur Rice and Pvt. Bruce Dunn are buried with full military honors on Jan. 3, 1945, at the 81st Division cemetery on the island of Angaur.

The battalion continued its work until the middle of February 1945, when it was ordered to prepare to move to Guam, in the Mariana Islands. After surmounting the inevitable transport impediments, the troops boarded the U.S.S. Johnson on February 27.

The 1887th left behind it an impressive record embracing the completion of one runway, two taxiways and 93 hard stands; erection of two tank forms; and one transit hotel ready for use.   When the U.S.S. Johnson plowed away from the shores of Angaur on the morning of Feb. 28, the men on board realized that they were leaving the scene of a successful mission.

Guam came into view on the morning of March 15, 1945, a cloudy day.   The seemingly barren hills in the background gave the islands a sinister appearance. Everyone was anxious to get off and give Guam the once-over.   Staff Sergeant Harold Washington made the following statement:

"Shortly after we reached Guam, I was made acting First Sergeant.   It was one of those things.   Talent was skimpy.   I was the only Soil Technician in the entire area.   They shuttled me from island to island periodically to test the soil.   There had been a high mortality rate among Soil Technicians.   I must have thought I was Emperor Jones and could only be wiped out with a silver bullet.   (Washington roared with laughter after making that statement.)   I did a great deal of structured reading while I was overseas.   I must have taken at least 30 correspondence courses.   Every 90 days I would report to the company warrant officer, who was our resident teacher for correspondence courses, to take a test in his presence on the material I had completed.   I took almost every course listed in the catalogues: history, literature, chemistry, and a great number of English courses.   I didn't take any physics courses because the Soil Technician School had been an accelerated truncated course in physics. I devoured

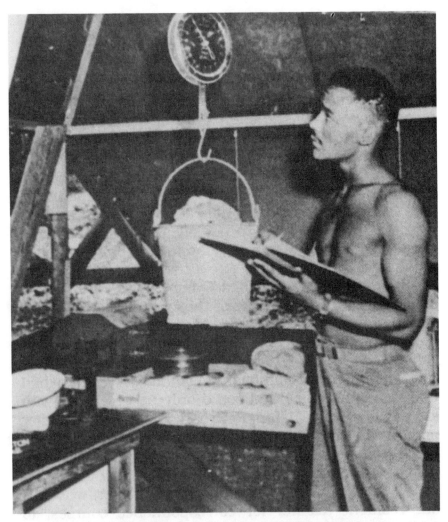

Soil Technician, 1st Sergeant Harold Washington.

all that material. Some people drink and chew gum; I read. All of my correspondence credits were mailed back to DuSable High School by the company warrant officer."

In the fall of 1945, at the time that First Sergeant Harold Washington was rushing through correspondence courses in the blazing sun over the Mariana Islands, his wife Dorothy Nancy was pursuing studies at Roosevelt College in Chicago, where she planned to complete courses to become an elementary school teacher.

Dorothy Nancy frequently wrote Harold love letters and also mentioned something about her academic progress at this new college founded without quotas for Negroes and other minorities. Harold salivated at the thought of a college without racial walls in his hometown. He cocked his hat to go there with hope of using the newly passed Servicemen's Readjustment Act, commonly known as the G.I. Bill of Rights. The Servicemen's Act offered veterans a living allowance, tuition fees, and money for books and supplies. In addition, there was the 52-20 Club, which allowed vets who couldn't find a job to collect $20 a week unemployment compensation for 52 weeks after getting out of the service.

On January 20, 1946, First Sergeant Harold Washington was discharged from the U.S. Army. Although Harold Washington frequently stated that he never dreamed of being Mayor of the City of Chicago, he never said that he was lacking the talent to do the job. The author feels it's proper to end this chapter with an article Harold wrote for the Army battalion newspaper. The article, "Ambition" appeared in the February 14, 1945 issue of the New World:

THE NEW WORLD   14 February 1945   PAGE 3

NO. 2

THE NEW WORLD
...ed and published by the person-
of an ENGINEER AVIATION BATTALION
#
...Somewhere in the Palaus***

EDITORIALS

If what shone afar so grand,
Turn to nothing in thy hand,
On again, the virtue lies
In the struggle, not the prize.

AMBITION

— T/3 Harold Washington —

History is saturated with biographies of empire building men. Caesar, Kahn, Napoleon, Washington, are names that are as familiar to us as our own. Henry Christopher was also an empire builder. Have you heard of him? Napoleon couldn't for...t him.

He rose from a condition of servitude to the exalted status of King of Haiti. Together, with Toussaint L'Ouverture, he defeated the vaunted legions of Napoleon. He changed Haiti from an obscure stop over to a famous trading port. His "Citadel" ...e proclaimed by many to be, the most ingenious edifice that was ever hatched, in the brain of man.

Christopher has been buried over a hundred years, but men of that ambitious character just don't die. They live on as inspiration to instill men with the desire to better themselves in life.

Ambition works as a stimulate to men, thus causing them to excell. Some men ...ipire to great deeds to pass their names down to posterity as useful members of their time, while others are satisfied to allow their lives to ebb away while they ...rely strive to enjoy themselves in any manner of trifling ways.

Surely the difficulties, wrongs, inequalities, and petty prejudices that ex...ist are no excuse to condone lethargy and lack of effort. We can take our cue from an ambitious man like Christopher and leave our children a better world than ...e found.

The sands of time run low. We must want, think, study, and act ——NOW.

Newspaper Article

Harold Washington, the Peoples' Mayor, being sworn in as Chicago's 42nd Mayor and the city's first black Mayor.

CORPORAL EDDIE MYLES

CHAPTER SEVENTEEN

"For Colored Only" Toilets Were In The Basement Of The Hospital

Eddie Myles was born in Detroit, Michigan on July 11, 1921. He and his brother moved to Chicago at the ages of 13 and 15 from their deceased mother's sister's home in St. Louis, Missouri at the request of their father. The father had not seen the boys in eleven years. The reason the 41-year-old man sent for his sons was to get an additional government relief supplement over and above his $55.00 per month Public Works Administration (PWA) check. The chemistry between the boys and their father was not strong. Both boys left home immediately after graduating from Wendell Phillips High School. Eddie got a single room down the street from his dad. About 3:15 p.m. on Sunday, December 7, 1941, Eddie Myles was sitting on the side of his bed doing his college homework when his favorite radio program was interrupted by the voice of a special announcer stating that Pearl Harbor had been attacked by Naval and Air Forces of the Empire of Japan. In Tokyo, the Japanese government declared war on the United States, Great Britain, and the Netherlands. On Monday, December 8, 1941, President Franklin D. Roosevelt appeared before a joint session of Congress and requested and received a declaration of war against Japan. Great Britain also declared war on Japan on December 8. Three days later Germany and Italy declared war on the United States and Congress in turn declared war on Germany and Italy.

Myles was a 20-year-old student at Wilson Junior College when America went to war. He had a job paying $10.00 per week at Greenbergs Pharmacy at 5901 South State Street. Out of his meager wages he paid $3.00 per week for room and board and only purchased raiment for his body when it was absolutely necessary. During the 1930s and early 40s three piece tailored suits were selling for $12.95 at the Wolhmuth Clothing Stores, and the very popular Tom McCann shoes could be purchased at $3.33.

In June 1942 the draft was heating up and Eddie Myles had to make a decision on electing to go to college for a second semester or going into the service. His very shallow pockets dictated that he could raise his standard of living by volunteering to join the Armed Forces. His first choice was the Navy, but they rejected him because of his poor vision. The Army recruiter on the other hand said, "If you can see that door that you just walked through you are our man."

On September 15, 1942, Eddie Myles became dog tag number 16125121, and a bona fide member of the United States Army. His standard of living was increased 150% in that his gross annual salary was raised from $520.00 to $600.00, plus three hot meals a day and a clean bunk at night. Uncle Sam's budget for his G.I. clothing allowance was almost unlimited in that it included: a garrison cap, cotton field cap, 1 field jacket, several pairs of wool and cotton socks, several changes of underwear for both summer and winter, 2 flannel shirts, 1 wool blouse, 2 khaki neckties, two sets of fatigues which included both blouse and trousers, 1 pair of wool trousers, 2 summer khaki cotton uniforms, 1 raincoat, 1 overcoat, and two pair of service shoes. All of the aforementioned items were issued by "Uncle Sam" at the Fort Custer Reception Center in Battle Creek, Michigan where his odyssey in the military began. In less than 72 hours after getting his clothing and a variety of immunization shots he was shipped from Fort Custer to Camp Lee, Virginia for eight weeks of basic training. From Lee he was shipped across the country to Fort Ord, California where he was prepped for duty overseas.

Eddie Myles recalls that when he boarded the liberty ship for a destination unknown, there were at least fifty armed military police on the boat standing approximately ten feet apart from stem to stern. Their presence on the ship was to minimize the number of soldiers who might attempt to jump ship and go over the hill. A day earlier, according to the garbage line, seventy five soldiers had jumped ship. Looking back fifty two years, Myles has indicated that he might have purposely missed that boat if he had known it was headed for the hot, steamy jungles of New Guinea.

The journey across the Pacific Ocean was eighteen frightening days on a zig zag route dodging enemy submarines and war ships. The landscape in New Guinea was strange but the people looked like American Negroes seven generations removed. The three to four month old babies looked just like cute colored American dolls. However, as they got older their skin aged with multiple wrinkles as a result of being exposed to

Fishing, hunting and dancing occupied the natives' time.

the extremely hot sun for long periods of time. It was so hot in New Guinea you could wash your clothes and hang them on a tree limb or bush and they would be bone dry in less than an hour. Fishing, hunting, and dancing seemed to occupy most of the natives' time.

The Japanese had landed on New Guinea in March 1942. They had not shown any propensity for killing or harming the natives in that their primary objective was to establish a base for attacking Australia, which was less than thirty five miles to the south. To keep the Allied Forces from getting too comfortable Japanese planes would drop several bombs on bright moonlit nights in the general area where Eddie Myles' 278th Service Battalion was entrenched. Fortunately only one member of a regiment of eight hundred men was killed by a bomb.

Since Corporal Eddie Myles was the company clerk, it was his responsibility to identify the deceased. The night before Myles was to go down to the morgue he did not sleep well because he was trying to imagine what his former comrade in arms from Hackensack, New Jersey would look like. To his surprise, the remains of the soldier looked like a mummy that had been dead for a thousand years. The only thing that placed this mummified body in the Twentieth Century was the Army dog tag which showed his serial number, name, and blood type.

In the Spring of 1944 the Japanese left in New Guinea were being pounded day and night from the air, and had been rendered incapable of doing anything more than suicidal resistance. Eddie Myles was on the edge of becoming a grain of sand in General Douglas Mac Arthur's most important action in the Pacific offensive.

Myles' service unit became a part of a 400 hundred to 500 hundred ship convoy streaming toward the Philippine Islands. According to Myles' estimate it took approximately 15 days to assemble all of the ships.

Gun boats were shooting over the heads of the Allied Troops for days to drive the Japanese back from the beaches so the troops could move in on landing barges. In the Fall of 1944, Field Marshall MacArthur waded ashore in the Philippines with the confidence of Moses walking across the dry bed of the Red Sea. This was the fruit of his having orchestrated the greatest amphibian landing ever at such a distance from operating bases and supplies. The General greeted his men with a wave of the same battered leaf-encrusted cap he had worn more than two years earlier when the Philippines had fallen to the enemy in 1942. At that time he said in his deep baritone voice: "I will return." He spoke to his men over the radio the day after he had victoriously waded ashore in October 1944. He simply roared: "I have returned." The American flag was raised on the beaches while machine guns and mortars raked the grass on the ground and blew the leaves off the trees.

While in the Philippines Eddie Myles became infected with a skin disease called Jungle Rot. The infection caused him to be hospitalized for approximately two months in the Philippines. He was sent back to the states on a hospital ship for a month's stay at Lettermans General Hospital in San Francisco, California. From Lettermans he was transferred to Walter Reed Hospital in Washington, D.C. It was at Walter Reed that returning sick and wounded colored war veterans were greeted with "FOR WHITES ONLY" signs on all the toilet facilities above the basement level.

Eddie Myles was discharged from the Army at the Walter Reed Hospital on November 15, 1945. He re-

Mess hall in the Philippines.

turned to Chicago, graduated from college with a Bachelors Degree, and in 1947 married Dorothy Harston, his high school sweetheart. Today Myles spends his time overseeing and enjoying the fruits of several very successful real estate investments.

LIEUTENANT COLONEL HAROLD THATCHER

CHAPTER EIGHTEEN

THE HEALERS AND ANGELS AT
FORT HUACHUCA, ARIZONA

D r. Harold Thatcher graduated from the University of Minnesota Medical School in December 1929. Although he was in the top 25% of his class, his opportunities for internship were limited to thirteen out of several thousand hospitals nationwide because of the color of his skin. The institutions available to Negroes were Provident Hospital in Chicago, Illinois; Freedmen's Hospital in Washington, D.C.; Harlem Hospital, New York; Lincoln Hospital, New York; Mercy Hospital, Philadelphia; St. Philips Hospital, Richmond, Virginia; Municipal Hospital No. 2, Kansas City, Missouri; Homer G. Philips Hospital and St. Mary's Infirmary, St. Louis, Missouri; Meharry Medical College, Georgia W. Hubbard Hospital, Nashville, Tennessee; Prairie View State College Hospital, Texas; and Dillard University, New Orleans, Louisiana. The aforementioned institutions did not accept any new interns except on July 1 of each year.

In January of 1930 the chairman of the Department of Pediatrics at the University of Minnesota accepted a lateral transfer to the University of Chicago Hospital. When he went back to Minnesota to visit his old clinic in early February he discovered that Thatcher had not been offered an internship.   He promised to get Thatcher an internship at the University of Chicago if he would accept it. Thatcher accepted the offer like a hungry dog accepts red meat. Two weeks after receiving the offer he got a letter inviting him to come to Chicago.

As a result of the close affiliation between the University of Chicago and Provident Hospital during that period, Thatcher's first assignment was with Dr. Theodore K. Lawless, the internationally distinguished dermatologist who was the Senior Attending Physician at Provident Hospital. Lawless also taught three mornings a week at the Northwestern University School of Medicine.

Dr. Harold Thatcher and Dr. T. K. Lawless met for the first time on Monday morning, February 24, 1930. Dr. Thatcher describes the event: "I had never heard of Dr. Lawless; I did not know anything about him. I got up that Monday morning feeling as fresh as a daisy, put on my white uniform, and paraded one block down the street to Provident Hospital, which fronted on East 51st Street across from Washington Park. I found Dr. Lawless in a large out-patient room with two tables and four nurses. I said good morning, the nurses did not respond, and Dr. Lawless did not open his mouth or acknowledge my presence even with a nod. I stood in the middle of the room and watched him examine several patients who were suffering with syphilis. After about an hour I began to feel I was in the

Dr. Theodore K. Lawless

wrong room and in everybody's way. When I started to walk toward the door, Dr. Lawless broke the chilled silence of the room and said: 'Young man do you think you have seen enough of this sort of stuff?' I said: "No, Sir!" Dr. Lawless snapped: "You learn by looking you know." I replied: "Yes, Sir!" The big man then gave me some smart talk and asked me if I knew how to give shots. I said: Yes, Sir. He then directed that I set up a booth and table and give between 30 and 40 out patient shots.

"After I finished a one year internship under Dr. Lawless he arranged for me to go back to the University of Chicago for two more years. I could not legally practice medicine, but at night I would go down to Dr. Lawless' private office and help him. The first year he gave me $500.00. The next year he gave me a little bit more. He frequently reminded me that his office was the place where you learn things. He was both right and also very difficult to work with. He gave me hell all the time. It got so bad I called my father in Minneapolis and told him about the conditions under which I was working. My dad asked me why didn't I leave. I told him that Dr. Lawless was a very good doctor and possibly the best in his field. My dad's response was curt; he said: If the devil had something that I wanted, I would stick with him until I got it.

"Dr. T. K. Lawless sent me to New York City for one year to study with some of his colleagues at two hospitals. When I returned to Chicago he said he wanted me to come into practice with him. After negotiating I agreed to stay with him and he promised to send me to Paris, France to study for one year. However, by September 1939 the German war machine had begun to move across Europe, and that automatically vetoed any chance I had to study in Paris."

In October 1940 the Surgeon General directed that Colored Medical Department officers be utilized only in units officered by colored, and that medical units with all whites remain lily white in keeping with the World War I Jim Crow strategy. Hospitals that served only colored should be staffed exclusively by colored personnel, including nurses. Colored and white medical officers could, if absolutely necessary, be used in the same hospital--provided that all supervising officers were white. There were colored hospital wards at both Fort Bragg, North Carolina and Camp Livingstone, Louisiana. Both of them were staffed by colored medi-

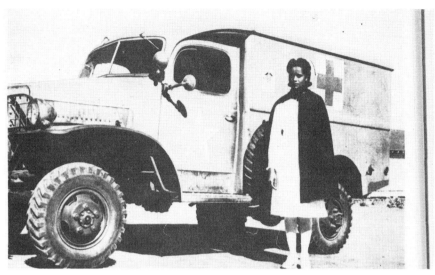

Lt. Margaret Key poses with an ambulance at Ft. Huachuca

Army Nurses at Station Hospital No. 1 Fort Huachuca, Arizona. *Reading down left column:* **Second Lieutenants, Mary G. Tyler, Olive Lucas, Lucille B. Miller, Joan L. Hamilton. Center: First Lieutenant Susan E. Freeman.** *Reading down right column:* **Second Lieutenants Chrystalee M. Maxwell, Bessie O. Hart, Bernice M. Batchelor, Margaret A. Key.**

Some of the nurses at Fort Huachuca, Arizona. *Left to right:*
**Bernice Batchelor, Los Angeles; Margaret A. Key, Philadel-
phia; Bessie O. Hart, Steelton, PA; Ellen L. Robinson, Hackensack, NJ; Joan Hamilton, St. Louis; Dorothy Branker, Bronx,
NY; Lillian Miller, Richmond Heights, MO; Elena Townsend,
Glen Cove, NY; Olive Lucas, Meadville, PA; Chrystallee Maxwell, Los Angeles; Mary G. Tyler, St. Louis**

cal officers and nurses. The overall scheme of the Surgeon General's plan was to minimize physical contact
between colored and white officers in such areas as entertainment, eating and housing. Although colored officers may have had top university credentials and
proven leadership abilities, these were qualities that
were never included in the Jim Crow equation.

Initially overseas colored nurses received assignments to hospitals where they could care for colored soldiers exclusively. The crisis came in Britain, when there were very few colored soldiers hospitalized. The colored nurses were ordered to care for German prisoners of war, which aroused so much resentment and hostility that the Chief Surgeon of the European Theater of Operations had to drop the Jim Crow policy and permit colored nurses to care for all Americans, regardless of race.

The 1940 Selective Service and Training Act found the Army playing catch up on its need to draft an increasing number of colored doctors and dentists in order to meet its new 10% racial quota under the Act. Dr. Thatcher was approached in the late winter of 1942 by Truman K. Gibson Jr., Civilian Aide to The Secretary of War, to join the Army and to become a part of a 1500 bed facility that was being built at Fort Huachuca, Arizona. Thatcher initially was offered a commission as a First Lieutenant. He wrote back and told Truman Gibson that he was going into another section of the Army because of some special work he was doing. The War Department wrote back and said he could come into the service as a Captain. Before Thatcher had a chance to respond he received another letter saying that he could join the Fort Huachuca Hospital staff as a Major. The doctor signed on after receiving a third promotion in a period of 19 days without donning a military uniform.

When Thatcher reached Huachuca in the early summer of 1942 they were still building the 1500 bed medical facility for colored soldiers. Thatcher and the other knowledgeable personnel had to order all of the equipment, such as hospital beds and the necessary machinery needed to run the hospital. It was better than a month before they could get into operation. However facility number 2, which was a 90 bed hospital, was in place for whites. It was used by white officers and enlisted men, their families and white civilian post personnel. When the word got around that the colored doctors were better prepared credentially and by skills than the white doctors, white patients began coming to Thatcher, who was an eminent skin specialist, and other board certified specialists at Station Hospital No. 1 in the afternoon between 3 and 5 pm. This period of the day considered "down time" for the physicians because they had finished their hospital rounds and had eaten lunch. Several wives of white officers told Thatcher that if he were white he would be a General.

Thatcher was not pleased in having to work at a hospital that had not been completed, in addition to being stationed in the middle of a desert surrounded by mountains and thirty-four miles from the nearest railroad station. Although his immediate boss was a home town friend, Colonel Midian O. Bousfield, Medical Director of the Supreme Liberty Life Insurance Company of Chicago, Special Health Director of the Julius Rosenwald (one of the founders of Sears) Fund and a member of the Chicago School Board, the Post Commander was an unreconstructed southerner from Tennessee.

To add insult to injury the Post Commander had electrical barbed wire fences installed around the dor-

**Colonel Midian O. Bousfield, Commanding Officer,
Station Hospital Number 1, Fort Huachuca, Arizona.**

mitories of white women who lived on the post, while
no such protection was provided for colored women living in the Jim Crow section of the Army base.

The Negro dormitories for married couples were un-painted plywood shacks that rivaled the worst slum housing in any back of the tracks ghetto. The living space per couple was seven feet square, each furnished with two Army cots and bedding.

The eleven couples who occupied the shelter all used the same sanitary facilities: one shower, one stool, two enameled iron sinks that served as face basins, and a laundry tub, also used in lieu of a bath tub. There were no facilities for cooking. The monthly rent was $12.00.

In comparison, white couples had spacious private rooms, adequate sanitary and laundry facilities, and bath tubs to supplement showers. There were kitchens where they could prepare their own meals or have them prepared. White Army wives had no complaints other than the isolation of the post.

Captain Grant Reynolds of New York City and the colored Chaplin at Fort Huachuca made the following observation:

"Negro soldiers will never forget the famous Hook and thousands of decent men will never forgive the War Department for allowing its existence. This little disease-infected area lay just south of the main entrance to the fort. It was comprised of ramshackle huts, tents, and vermin-infested adobe structures. This disgraceful community did a thriving, though deadly, business in prostitution. Electric lights, pavement, running water, or any other signs of sanitation were entirely unknown. Yet this pest hole of venereal disease was allowed to flourish at the very front door of the Home of the Negro Soldier."

Reynolds further stated that:

"Due to his deplorable environmental conditions the Negro, more than any other segment of the American population, has suffered from the ravages of social diseases. The War Department has gone to great expense and considerable effort to protect its soldiers from this deadly killer. Fort Huachuca colored soldiers apparently did not come within the purview of this program."

The GU Wards (where venereal cases were treated) were over taxed because the post authorities allowed their sex dens to operate at the front door to the living room of church going, God fearing colored men and women who were forced to live in a desert fortress cut off from civilization because they volunteered or were drafted to fight and win a war to make democracy a reality on two fronts, at home for themselves and abroad.

Dr. Thatcher indicated that for efforts to control venereal disease imported from Mexico to be successful, it would be necessary to send a team of doctors down to the Mexico border on weekends and require physical inspection of every soldier reentering the United States.

The following case related by Dr. Stephen Stanford of Philadelphia, the venereal control officer at Fort Huachuca, to the late Enoch Waters, his childhood friend and War Correspondent for the Chicago Defender and the author of the autobiography, American Dairy, is a good example of the real-life dramas that took place:

The G.I. was the "clap" victim of a young hooray girl for whom he expressed undying love.

"Why didn't you use a rubber?" the physician asked.

"Oh I couldn't do a thing like that, sir. She ain't no whore and I am in love with her."

"Maybe so, but you see she's got gonorrhea. What's her name? Where does she live?"

"I won't tell you, sir. She's a nice girl from a nice family. It wouldn't be right."

"But she needs medical treatment which we can see that she gets. If she isn't treated, it will get worse and you can't make love to her anymore."

"I'll handle it myself."

"Besides," the doctor added as a second thought, "she might infect someone else."

The young GI was indignant. "She loves only me. She don't mess around like some of the other girls."

"Well, just to play safe you ought to use a rubber from now on."

"I could never do that with her. It would be an insult."

Part of the medical officers and nurses at Ft. Huachuca including Major Thatcher, *(3rd from right).*

More medical officers and nurses from Ft. Huachuca including Colonel Bousfield, *(in forefront).*

Additional medical officers at Station Hospital No. 1 standing in formation with Col. Bousfield *(in forefront).*

"Maybe so, but it would also keep her from getting pregnant. Did you ever think of that?"

"It wouldn't matter. We're going to be married."

The medical officer shook his head in disgust. "I don't know what to do about you guys."

Fort Huachuca had the only fully staffed colored hospital in the Army. Every one of the doctors were board certified in his specialty. As of February 1, 1943, 131 Negro nurses had been enrolled in the Army. Sixty nine percent were stationed at Fort Huachuca. The 131 nurses were distributed as follows: Fort Huachuca 90, Camp Bragg 13, Camp Livingstone 15, Tuskegee 13.

Medical officers and nurses at Ft. Huachuca.

Second Lieutenant Nora Green, a nurse at the station hospital of the Tuskegee Flying School, was brutally beaten by several white Montgomery police on September 12, 1942 because she boarded a bus that was otherwise occupied by whites. Both of her eyes were blackened and her nose was broken. She was thrown into a jail cell and charged with being intoxicated when it was known by her associates that she never drank anything stronger than a coke.

Only 500 colored nurses out of 50,000 served during World War II. The Navy had only four colored nurses out of 11,000 during the same period. The Marines had none.

After Dr. Harold Thatcher was discharged from the Army in 1946, he renewed his practice of medicine with Dr. T. K. Lawless until Lawless died on May 1, 1974. Dr. Lawless respected and trusted Dr. Thatcher's judgement in that he made him co-executor of his estate with the Continental Bank.

Dr. Thatcher is still practicing medicine in the noble tradition of Dr. T. K. Lawless. All patients, rich and poor, are treated alike on a first-come, first-served basis.

1st LIEUTENANT MILTON B. DEAS

CHAPTER NINETEEN

YOU CAN STAND IN THE WELL OF THE BUS, BUT YOU CAN'T SIT DOWN

Milton B. Deas was born in Chicago, Illinois on February 25, 1920. His father, Harry B. Deas, joined the Chicago Police Department five years before he was born and subsequently became the second Negro in the history of the city to reach the rank of Captain of an ARPA Station.

Milton was a multi-talented musician who attended DuSable High School with such entertainment greats as Nate "King" Cole, Fred "Red Foxx" Sanford, Dorothy Donegan, Thomas Rigsby, John Young, Martha Davis, Austin Powell and a host of others who gained fame in night clubs, recordings, theaters, television and movies.

Although Milton had put a couple of years of college under his belt at both Howard University and the University of Wisconsin he wanted to be a policeman like his father. His dad wanted him to be something other than a cop. After some months of debate, Milton's father came up with an acceptable compromise. The Selective Service Act had just been passed in September

1940 making it mandatory for every physically fit man between the ages of 21 and 35 to serve one year in the military. In the light of the military mandate, the senior Deas told his son that he should get the one year in the Army behind him and thereby avoid interrupting the continuity of his record once he joined the Police Department.

On October 3, 1940, Milton B. Deas submitted himself for service with the 8th Illinois Infantry Guards. The 8th Illinois Infantry was activated into the regular Army on January 5, 1941 as the 184th Field Artillery. They were shipped to Fort Custer, Michigan in late De-

Home of the Eighth Infantry Regiment.

cember 1940 with the understanding that they would only be there for one year.

The schedule at Fort Custer was filled with training activity and the weeks rolled into months very fast. The officers and men of the 184th were packing their gear because the twelve months of mandatory service had dwindled to just a few highly anticipated days. On Sunday, shortly before noon, December 7, 1941, Milton was lounging on his bunk and listening to the radio when the voice of a special announcer broke the tranquility of the lazy, hazy morning with the bone shaking news that the Japanese Airforce had bombed Pearl Harbor. All bets were off for going home.

Young Milton Deas realized that he was going to be in the Army for the duration so he decided to apply for Officers Candidate School. He was accepted and sent to the Armored Force School at Fort Knox, Kentucky. The classroom sessions and the mess facilities were integrated. The housing was segregated in that they stuffed 13 colored O.C.S. candidates into double deck bunks in a squad room that was intended to only accommodate six individuals comfortably Army style. A week before Deas was to graduate from Fort Knox he and six other colored candidates were kicked out of school because they, in the eyes of Charley (white training instructors), did not display leadership ability.

In March 1943 Deas reapplied for Officers Candidate School with the blessings of Colonel Theopholus Mann, his Commanding Officer and an excellent lawyer in civilian life. Deas wanted to go to the Field Artillery School at Fort Sill, Oklahoma. He was told by Colonel Mann that there were no openings. However, the Colonel told him there was space in the Tank Destroyer School at Camp Hood, Texas. He asked Milton

Lt. Colonel Theopholus Mann,
Commanding Officer

if he would like to go. Deas replied in the affirmative because he wanted to prove to himself and the Colonel that he was made out of the kind of material that warranted him being an officer in the Army of the United States.

Camp Hood was just a few miles from a small old town that still had dirt streets and board walks in the business district along with hitching posts for the horses. It would have made an excellent site for a movie like "High Noon" with Gary Cooper. The only thing missing was the gunman in the white hat coming out of the swinging doors of a saloon with both guns blazing.

Deas *(in 3rd row, 3rd seat from left)* **in a picture of the OCS graduating class of October 1943 at Camp Hood, Texas.**

Camp Hood was unlike Fort Knox in that Deas was the only non-white member of the June 1943, Officers Candidate School class. He was housed in the same barracks as the other candidates. He was respected by most of the men because he was a First Sergeant.

After graduation Milton Deas decided to take a bus down to San Antonio, Texas to visit a young lady who subsequently became his wife. When he got on the bus, the driver was so congenial that Milton decided to sit down behind him and talk. Before he could spit three words out of his mouth the bus driver told him he had to go to the back of the bus. Deas complied. When the bus reached Brownsville it emptied. There was nobody else going to San Antonio but Milton Deas.

At this point the bus driver called Deas to the front of the bus and said: "I feel bad as a man. You are going overseas to fight for me, and I am sitting back here safe and secure driving a bus and I tell you and others like you that you got to sit at the back of the bus because of the color of your skin. I am ashamed for my country and I hope you don't hold anything against me as an individual."

Down the road a piece the driver bent the rules after commiserating and called Deas back to the front of the bus a second time and told him he could stand in the well of the door and talk to him if he wished but he could not sit.

When he reached San Antonio he took his wife to be out to dinner and then to a small theater down on Commerce Street. He never went back to the theater because he found it distasteful to pay for a ticket at the booth in front of the theater and then have to go around to the back and up the fire escape, like a thief in the night, to the colored section which was commonly called the Peanut Gallery.

On August 3, 1943 Milton B. Deas and Mary Etta Black of San Antonio, Texas got married just four days before his battalion shipped out for overseas.   Deas was an officer of Company A of the 614th Battalion. The top five officers were white and the remainder of the staff were Negroes, including all of the Company officers.   The 614th became attached to the 103rd Division on December 7th.   It was committed to action on November 28 when it relieved the 705th Tank Destroyer Battalion.

Members of an armored tank division spearhead an attack.

On December 1st, the first day on the line, a platoon from the 614th Company C scored three direct hits on enemy-held pill boxes North of Bourges, France.   The Germans raised a white flag, but when the patrol approached they opened fire.   The colored soldiers in the Tank Destroyer reacted with a "we will take no prison ers" mentality and resumed firing.   The German soldiers responded by retreating out of their pill boxes.

Their action before Climbach, France, in which the platoon lost half of its men, killed or wounded, enabled the Task Force to capture the town and force the enemy to retreat from Climbach and retire to the Siegfried Line.

For its action at Climbach, France, the 3rd Platoon, Company C, and 614th Tank Destroyer Battalion received the Distinguished Unit Citation. It was the first colored ground unit to receive the honor in World War II. In addition to a Distinguished Service Cross for Lieutenant Charles L. Thomas of Detroit, Michigan,

Captain Charles L. Thomas, 614th Tank Destroyer Battalion, who won the DSC for heroism at the battle of Climbach, France, in 1944.

who was a Tank Commander, the platoon also earned four Silver Stars, two of them awarded posthumously, and nine Bronze Stars. After Lieutenant Thomas was carried off the field wounded, Technician Fifth Grade Robert W. Harris displayed courage, above and beyond the call of duty, when he drove a truck loaded with live ammunition across an open battle field to keep the Units' guns in action. When Major General Charles T. Haffner Jr., Commander of the 103rd Division, personally pinned their decorations on two officers and nine enlisted men at a ceremony on December 28, the Unit declared it "a great morale factor for our troops."

Milton B. Deas was discharged from the service as a First Lieutenant on May 7, 1947 after serving in the Occupational Army in Europe with the 761st Tank Battalion. After leaving the service Deas immediately took steps to fulfill his childhood dream of becoming a Chicago policeman like his father. He served on the force from December 1947 to February 25, 1983. He worked his way up from a Foot Patrolman to Commander of Detectives Area #2.

JUDGE EARL STRAYHORN
FORMER U.S. ARMY 1st LIEUTENANT

CHAPTER TWENTY

A FLY IN A BOTTLE
OF BUTTERMILK

Earl Strayhorn was inducted into the Armed Forces on October 14, 1941 after completing a cursory physical examination at an induction station located on Van Buren near State Street in Chicago, Illinois. Following the brief swearing in ceremony he and approximately 100 other young colored men were immediately transported on the Illinois Central Railroad to Fort Custer, in Battle Creek, Michigan for eight weeks of basic training. The basic training was aborted, without the benefit of rifle training, after three weeks because a special order came down from the Sixth Area Headquarters directing that a detachment of 45 men be transferred immediately to Tuskegee, Alabama.

Strayhorn, the acting leader in charge, and the 44 other new soldiers were greeted at Tuskegee by a cold Alabama wind. The barracks at Tuskegee had not been completed, therefore, the three week old recruits spent their first ten nights in Alabama sleeping under canvas tents equipped with wood burning stoves and some freshly cut logs that had not been aged for burning. Each morning one man in each tent had to knock the soot off of the spark deflectors in order to get a proper draft for the simmering ashes as well as prevent the sparks from igniting the untreated tent material that the Army was using at that period.

Since there were no officers on the base, Strayhorn continued to act as a leader for the 44 men. He held that leadership role until late November when a contingent of men arrived who had been in training at Chanute Field in Rantoul, Illinois specifically for the Tuskegee Experiment. The men from Chanute had not been at Tuskegee 10 days when the Japanese bombed Pearl Harbor on December 7, 1941.

Shortly after Pearl Harbor the Military Police organizational table was put in place under Commanding Officer Captain George W. Webb. The Captain appointed Earl Strayhorn as his First Sergeant, a position that he held until mid-February 1942 when he left Tuskegee to go to the Field Artillery Officers Candidate School at Fort Sills, Oklahoma.

At Fort Sills, Strayhorn was housed in a tent with five other O.C.S. Candidates. "I was a fly in a bottle of buttermilk," he states. In other words, he was the only Negro in his tent. Strayhorn's tent mates were from Alabama, Texas and Brooklyn, New York. He discovered after a very brief period that the white boy from New York was more racist than the boys from the Confederate states.

There were only two Negro candidates, in addition to Strayhorn, out of a class of two hundred; all 3 gradu-

Commanding Officer Captain George W. Webb, talks to MPs.

ated in the top ten percent of the class. After receiving his commission, Strayhorn was sent back to Fort Custer, Michigan where he was assigned to the 184th Field Artillery Regiment, commanded by all-Negro officers. The Regimental Commander of the 184th was Colonel Anderson F. Pitts from Chicago, Illinois. In the 27 years that Strayhorn was in the military, on active duty or in the National Guard, he never served directly under any officer who was not Negro. His experience is very unique when one considers that the philosophy of the United States Army was based on the false premise that the best leaders of Negro troops were white officers from the South.

**Regimental Commander,
Colonel Anderson F. Pitts**

It was the customs of the South that caused Northern colored troops numerous racial problems. An example is a race riot that came within a single gun shot of taking place at Camp Forrest, Tennessee over segregated seating in a post theater. Lieutenant Earl Strayhorn was both present and accounted for and he describes the situation as follows:

"When we arrived at Camp Forrest, Tennessee from Camp Gordon at Augusta, Georgia, the first thing we heard was how bad colored troops were being treated in reference to using any facilities outside of the designated Colored Area on the Post. All the colored units, with the exception of the WACs, were insulated in one section of the camp, as if by contact they would give their white brothers in arms a severe case of 'black plague'.

"On the 184th's first evening in Camp Forrest one of our First Sergeants ordered his men to line up in full Class A Uniform at 6:00 p.m. and march to the theater where they all bought tickets and took seats everywhere in the house except the area marked 'FOR COLORED ONLY'. The commissioned colored officers were not going to let the enlisted men out do them, therefore they integrated the white officers' section. The white military police responded by ordering 250 colored officers and men out of the theater at gun point. After they were ejected from the theater they were made to line up in a drainage ditch by the side of the road under the muzzles of sub-machine guns pointed at their heads.

"One week later, the same Post Theater was showing a 4-Star picture entitled, 'This Land is Mine', which featured Charles Laughton, and included a scene of Laughton reading The Bill of Rights. A large number of officers and men wanted to see the picture so we decided we would repeat our earlier movie theater integration sit-in. This time the scene was changed because the Post Commander, Colonel M. F. Waltz, came to the theater with 50 Military Police armed with Thompson Machine Guns at the ready in the event things got out of control. The MPs remained outside of the theater. The Colonel had the lights turned on and he addressed First Lieutenant Robin E. L. Washington, one of our officers who was sitting on the end seat. The Colonel said: 'Lieutenant don't you see that section marked COLORED OFFICERS?' Lieutenant Washing-

ton replied: 'Yes, Sir.   The Colonel then said: 'Why
aren't you sitting there?'   Lieutenant Washington recoiled: 'Well, Sir, when I was commissioned I did not
see anything on my commission from the President of
the United States designating where I should sit.'   The
Colonel turned beet red and blustered: 'On this Post,
where there is a designation for COLORED OFFICERS,
you will sit there.'   Lieutenant Washington retorted:
'No, Sir!   I will remain, by your leave or without your
leave.   I will not move out of this section marked Officers.   The Colonel then proceeded to ask each individual officer, on two contiguous rows of seats, the same
questions and he got the same replies mouthed by
Lieutenant Washington from each Negro officer, without exception.

"The Colonel, with the snap of a wipe, ordered his
Aide to bring in the Military Police.   The MPs lined up
on the left and right aisles with their Thompson Machine Guns at the ready.   They had encircled the Negro officers.   One of our enlisted men saw what was
happening and he ran back to the Unit Area and alert-
ed Lieutenant Colonel Marcus H. Ray about the im-
pending crisis.   Lieutenant Colonel Ray arrived in minutes after the MPs had positioned themselves and we
had refused to move.   The Lieutenant Colonel came
down the aisle to where we were seated and said: 'Officers of the 184th follow me.'   We all got up and followed our Colonel.   He took us to the theater office
where he met with the Post Commander, Colonel
Waltz, who was a bird Colonel and out-ranked our
Lieutenant Colonel, who wore a silver oak leaf.   Colonel Waltz said: 'Lieutenant Colonel Ray, I am going to

file charges against you for inciting a riot.' He filed charges with the 2nd Army Commander, Lieutenant

Lieutenant Colonel Marcus H. Ray

General Lesley J. McNair. The General neither sustained nor dismissed the charges, neither did he convene a court martial. However, he did relieve Colonel Waltz of his command. Waltz was subsequently killed in the North Africa Campaign. Today I still wonder what would have happened if Colonel Ray had not come to the theater that night."

The officers involved in the second theater incident were: First Lieutenants John A. Rector, David W. Pelkey, Lawrence Langford, Robbin E. L. Washington, Welton I. Taylor, and Ernest Davenport; Second Lieutenants Byron Minor, James Dunn, Ernest V. Williams and Warrant Officer, Milton J. Winfield Jr.

After the first theater sit-in the 184th Field Artillery Regiment was persona-non grata at Camp Forrest, Tennessee. They were reassigned to Camp Gordon, which was just a few miles outside of Augusta, Georgia. It was at Camp Gordon that the 931st Field Artillery Battalion, a descendant of the old 8th Illinois Infantry, was converted into an engineer combat (hard labor) battalion.

The break up was a grim scene that brought tears from the eyes of hardened soldiers. Lieutenant Colonel Marcus H. Ray, from Chicago, the tall and soldierly Commander of the battalion who had labored long hours to qualify his unit for combat duty, stood mute and saddened as he watched the troop train leave with some of the best men of the battalion. Some of the soldiers who were left standing at the rail siding wept uncontrollably.

The officers left behind, waiting for further orders, were the following:

Lieutenant Colonel Marcus H. Ray, Commanding, Chicago; Major Edward D. Wimp Jr., Executive, Chicago; Major Bennett G. Gray, Chicago; Major Percy R. Turnley, Chicago; Captain Claude C. Clark, Chicago; Captain David W. Pelkey, Chicago; Captain Harold L. Miles, Chicago; Captain Don V. Estill, Chicago; First Lieutenant Scott K. Clease, Chicago; First Lieutenant Webb Threet, Chicago; 2nd Lieutenant Byron C. Minor, Chicago; 2nd Lieutenant Earl E. Strayhorn, Chicago; 2nd Lieutenant Albert A. Loving, Chicago; 1st Lieutenant John A. Rector, Pittsburgh; 1st Lieutenant Lester H. Brownlee, Evanston, Illinois; 1st Lieutenant

Major Edward D. Wimp Jr.   **Captain Claude C. Clark**

Robbin E. L. Washington, Huntington, West Virginia; 1st Lieutenant Samuel M. Love, Detroit; 2nd Lieutenant Herman M. Bell, Philadelphia; 2nd Lieutenant Clark Lowe, Palestine, Texas; 2nd Lieutenant James F. Dunn, New York City; 2nd Lieutenant Marion H. Smith, San Antonio, Texas; 2nd Lieutenant LaVon E. Smith, Austin, Texas; 2nd Lieutenant Ernest V. Williams, Toledo, Ohio; 1st Lieutenant Clifford R. Moore, Philadelphia; 1st Lieutenant Steve Davis, Chicago; and 1st Lieutenant Marvin O. Parker, Baltimore, Maryland.

Captain David W. Pelkey, one of the officers left standing by the railroad tracks, states the following:

"They successfully broke up the enlisted men and officer aspect of the 931st Field Artillery. However, the officers of the 931st received orders to report to the 92nd Division at Fort Huachuca, Arizona."

Pelkey continues, "The 92nd Division troops were 100 percent colored whereas the officers were all white, with the exception of a few Negro Second Lieutenants. There were no colored Unit Commanders until we got there. I took over the battery with the same officers that had been with me from Fort Custer, to Camp Gordon, to Camp Forrest and back to Camp Gordon. We replaced almost all of the white officers from Lieutenant Colonels down to Second Lieutenants."

Since there was an unwritten rule that no white officer could serve under a Negro superior, the turnover at Fort Huachuca can best be understood in that context.

A later example took place in 1946, when the 477th, under Colonel B. O. Davis Jr., moved to Lockbourne Army Air Force Base in Ohio. This event marked the first time Negro officers were permitted to administer an Army Air Force Base or any other kind of military facility in the continental United States without the immediate supervision of white officers.

Strayhorn was shipped out of Fort Huachuca to a port of debarkation in Virginia with the 92nd Division in September 1944. When they landed in Naples, Italy they immediately went into the battle line during the final days of the battle for Rome. Prior to reaching Rome the Allies and the Germans agreed that Rome was to be a free and open city and therefore would not become a part of the war. Rome was by-passed.

The 92nd Division fought in Italy until the German resistance cracked just above Florence. Up to that point the 92nd had been fighting at a disadvantage in the mountains.   Out of the mountains, they poured down into the Italian farmland.   The flat terrain allowed the Allies to out maneuver the Germans with the Allies' overwhelming superior power in personnel and material.

On February 22, 1946 Strayhorn was discharged from the Army with battle ribbons and the rank of First Lieutenant.   He immediately entered law school, and today is the presiding judge of the first Municipal District of the Circuit Court of Cook County, Illinois.

Judge Strayhorn received his undergraduate degree from the University of Illinois, Urbana, Illinois in 1941. His Juris Doctor degree was earned from DePaul University College of Law in 1948.

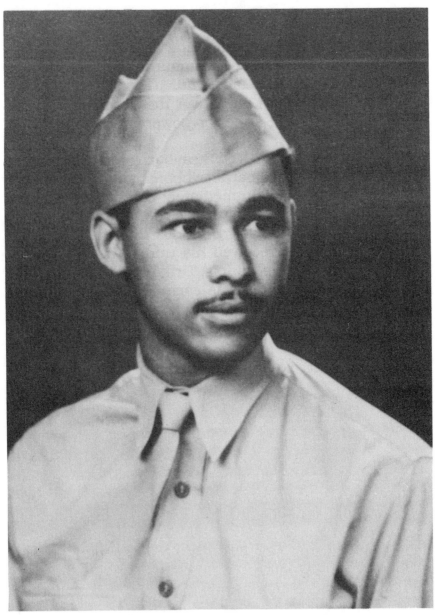

SERGEANT FRANK W. GARDNER

CHAPTER TWENTY-ONE

This G.I. Ate Out Of A Plate
Reserved For The Coloreds

Frank W. Gardner was born in Chicago, Illinois on June 12, 1923 at St. Luke's Hospital. In the 1920s colored folks entered and left that institution through a back door, which fronted on the Illinois Central Railroad yard, as opposed to the front door which faced upscale Michigan Boulevard. The back door mentality did not go out of fashion with the Roaring Twenties Charleston dance, because in the 1940s Frank entered the United States Army in the same Jim Crow style as our fathers did more than two decades earlier.

Gardner became a volunteer in the Army Reserve Corp in November 1942 while he was still a student at the Chicago Teachers College. He thought that volunteering would enable him to stay in school until he graduated. He was wrong. The Army requested the pleasure of having Dog Tag #16145793 report for active duty and bring the neck of the wearer along in September 1943. Frank Gardner and a hundred other colored recruits were shipped to Fort Custer, Michigan where they were processed and then sent to various camps throughout the United States. Gardner was sent to Aberdeen Proving Ground, Maryland for his basic training.

While at Aberdeen he was selected to participate in the Army Special Training Program (ASTP) as a result of the high score he made on the service men's aptitude test. After completing his basic training he was shipped from Aberdeen Proving Ground to Prairie View College in Texas to study engineering as an ASTP student.

Enroute to Texas, Jim Crow slapped Gardner on both sides of his face. The first slap came when he was told he had to separate from his white traveling companions and sit in the soot and dust-filled, sardine packed "For Colored Only" car. This car was located at the front of the train next to the coal car and the hand fired locomotive. The second slap came in New Orleans, Louisiana when he was told at the train station that the only place he could use his Army meal voucher was in the kitchen. Through the kitchen swinging doors he could see the white soldiers, who had left Aberdeen Proving Ground with him, eating in style in what appeared, through his eyes, to be the Taj Mahal of dining rooms.

Frank Gardner was a 19 year old kid who had never been outside of Chicago. He was mentally hurt but not permanently damaged because of the Jim Crow experience. Although he could not understand the rationale for racism, he simply followed orders like a good soldier and swallowed it.

Prairie View College was a product of Jim Crow but it was not racist because it was an all-Negro school. It had an atmosphere similar to the West Chesterfield Community he was raised in on the southeast side of Chicago. However, like all good things, the Army Special Training Program was soon discontinued, and Frank and several hundred other high I.Q. boys were sent to join the 92nd Division on maneuvers in Shreveport, Louisiana. They went from nice clean sheets in college dorms to sleeping in tents on cots in the hot steamy Louisiana swamps. The maneuvers in Louisiana was the Army's 102 preparatory course for going overseas.

The 92nd Division returned to their home base at Fort Huachuca, Arizona after they completed their field maneuvers. Frank Gardner marched up and down the Arizona hills for two more months before the Division pulled up stakes and headed for Newport News, Virginia, a port of embarkation. It was in Newport where the all-Negro 92nd ran into racial problems with the military police. Many of the men had taken on a fatalistic attitude prior to going overseas. Newport was a powder keg. The slightest slight would ignite a fight.

Without suffering any fatalities in Newport, the 92nd Division, with the exception of Battery A, boarded a liberty ship whose destination was unknown prior to leaving the port. Frank noted that all of the top ranking Army officers were white. There were some colored lieutenants and maybe a hand full of captains. A few Negro lieutenant colonels and majors were aboard the ship but Frank did not see them. When the boat docked in Naples, Italy the German and Italian soldiers had passed out posters that the Negro Division was coming and that they were savage rapists of the worst kind. The white American soldiers who pre-

The infantry men of the 92nd in the hills of Italy.

ceded them had also successfully indoctrinated people in the Pacific, England, North Africa, and throughout Europe with the same kind of racist propaganda.

There were plenty of prostitutes roaming the streets of Naples. Some of them were racist in that they would entertain brown and light complexioned Negroes but would have nothing to do with ebony skinned soldiers. According to the whores, they feared reprisals from their own people and other whites if they socialized with pure black men.

After leaving Naples, Frank Gardner went to war in one of Italy's many hills. The reality of battle had not sunk into his consciousness. He recalls running up a hill firing away at several fleeing enemy soldiers. His only thought was "if my girlfriend could see me now", that is, until one of the German soldiers turned around and started shooting at him. Frank then unloaded his rifle in the direction of the German soldier, who died instantly after being hit.

After this encounter a more mature Frank Gardner began to reflect on the fact that he had killed someone he did not even know. The man he had killed had never done anything to him; they had never even exchanged angry words. The bullets they fired at each other were not the rubber kind that was intended to bounce off your body; they were designed to kill. The victims of war didn't get up and dust themselves off and walk away like they do after shooting a battle scene in a movie. War was real and Frank Gardner really began to recognize it when his comrades began to fall dead in front of his eyes. He lost his boyhood friend Vernon Blanchard in the European Theater of

War. The remains of this fine young soldier were not found until after the victory in Europe in May 1945. War was mankind's worst invention.

Frank Gardner returned to the United States on an aircraft carrier. When the ship reached the United States and the soldiers prepared to debark, two lines were formed, one for white soldiers and the other for Negroes. It was at this point that Frank awakened to the realization that he was back home in the country that went to war to make democracy a reality for all the citizens of the world.

Sergeant Frank Gardner during rest and relaxation in Rome, Italy in the Spring of 1944.

In 1946 Staff Sergeant Frank Gardner re-entered the Chicago Teachers College and graduated with a B.A. degree. He subsequently received his Masters and Doctorate degrees, while working in every level of the Chicago Public School system. Ultimately he became President of the Chicago School Board of Education, during the administration of Mayor Harold Washington.

DR. ARTHUR M. BRAZIER,
FORMER ARMY STAFF SERGEANT

CHAPTER TWENTY-TWO

ARMY DEGRADATION DURING WWII
DAMAGED THE NEGRO SOLDIERS' PSYCHE

Dr. Arthur M. Brazier is a veteran of World War II. He was drafted into the Army in Chicago, Illinois and shipped out to Camp Custer on October 26, 1942. In Camp Custer he was transformed from Jody (nick-name for civilian) to Private Brazier, given the metal dog tags numbered 36386393, and instructed to wear them around his neck twenty-four hours a day for the duration of the war.

From Camp Custer he was shipped South to several camps, starting with an Air Force Base near Tallahassee, Florida, and then to Ten Mile Station just outside of Charleston, South Carolina. Private Brazier describes the racial climate in the Army and its Southern environs as bad. They were the things that caused him to totally dislike the Army. He was put into all-Negro Jim Crow units that were officered completely by white men. Although he had been born and raised in Chicago, a city with the reputation of being the most segregated city in America, it was the first time that he had come face-to-face with total segregation. He had experienced racism in Chicago but he was not fully aware of its power because it was much more subtle.

Private Brazier's bus ride in an off-the-map town outside of Chattanooga, Tennessee was among the most humiliating experiences he bore while in the armed services. It was on the bus that the realization came starkly to him that he could not sit in any seat except those designated for coloreds at the very back of the bus. What galled him most about sitting in the back of the bus was that he had to do it wearing an American Army uniform. An adjustment in his life-style was mandatory if he was to survive in the mid and deep South because he did not know where he could go and what he should do outside of the Negro ghettos.

Halls, Tennessee was totally off limits to Negro soldiers. You would put your life in harms way if out of ignorance you stopped someone to ask for directions. Down the road there was another town called Ripley, where there was a small Negro neighborhood. At 10 o'clock p.m. the sheriff would drive through the streets blowing a whistle which was the signal for colored soldiers to get off the streets or leave town. Those who did not want to go back to camp could go to the woods on the outskirts of town where a young colored entrepreneur had set up a make shift dance hall.

On the Army air base in Dyersburg, Tennessee colored soldiers could go to the white Post Exchange but they were humiliated in that they were treated like non-persons. You could be first in line at the counter but you were always the last served. You were a frozen chocolate popsicle until the white soldiers' needs had been fulfilled.

You were forced to undergo the humiliation that was dumped on you at the white Post Exchange because the colored Post Exchange had very little merchandise except 3.2 beer and smokes. In addition, the facility was not big enough to laugh in.

Private Arthur Brazier knew that being humiliated without cause, except the color of his skin, was poisonous to his soul. He attempted to minimize the humiliation by staying on the Army base where mistreatment of colored soldiers was a wee bit less severe than it was in the surrounding Southern towns and cities.

Ignorance of Southern customs was no excuse for innocent behavior on the part of a Northern colored soldier in South Carolina. Brazier's Company Commander sent him and another soldier to the train station in the town of Florence, South Carolina to pick up two barrack bags that had been left there by a recruit who had been transferred into their Company. The train station had two sides and in the center was a circular office where the station master was seated adjacent to a small baggage room. Brazier walked into the station and told the Station Master that he was there to pick up two barrack bags. As he spoke, he was pointing at the two bags. The Station Master said: "You are on the wrong side." Brazier innocently explained: "There are the bags right there two feet from you. You can give them to me now." The Station Master turned beet red.

There was a minute of silence, then in an amplified voice he said: "Get out of here and go around to the other side." Brazier, acting as if he did not hear the command, said: "Why don't you give me those bags right there?" By this time the expression on the train master's face was as ferocious as a mad bull dog. The sight of the man's face dictated to Brazier that he and his companion solider should do an about face and go around to the other side.

The Station Master had a two minute transformation. When Brazier approached him from the other side he was as polite as a deacon on Sunday morning. As a matter of fact, the Station Master acted as if he had never seen Brazier before. When Brazier asked for the barrack bags, the station master, in the politest tone, said: "Oh, yes! Here they are," and handed the bags to Brazier with a smile.

Private Brazier witnessed a similar transformation by a white dentist when he was preparing to go overseas. He was having his final dental examination and the dentist had pulled a tooth and part of it had broken off in his gums. "The dentist was digging around and he began to hurt me," Brazier said. "I raised up and the dentist shouted, 'Lay back down there Nigger'. My God, I felt like I had been shot," Brazier exclaimed. He laid back down; blood was streaming out of the side of his mouth and the suction pump was working overtime. When the dentist completed his work, Arthur Brazier was permitted to get out of the dental chair and straighten himself up. At that time the dentist was as polite and thoughtful as one could possibly expect. He acted as if he had never used the "N" word.

The shock of that dental experience 50 years ago still lingers in Brazier's mind as if it had happened yesterday. As he told the author the story, Brazier explained that his body was heating up with the same sense of humiliation he had experienced five decades ago.

Brazier's statement is important in helping to bring some understanding of the deep psychological trauma that colored soldiers had to go through in the military service during World War II. The mentality that was portrayed in the movie "Glory" as representing the relationship in 1862 between Negro soldiers and white officers was still in place in 1962, one hundred years later.

When Brazier's division received its notice to go overseas the men literally jumped for joy because this appeared to be their only exit out of the South. They realized that they would be facing some dangerous situations; however, many preferred the danger of war in distant lands to the humiliation they received at home.

It is interesting that five days before Brazier's group reached India, the white officers called all the Negro soldiers on deck to hear a long lecture about how the colored soldiers should not discuss anything about discrimination and segregation in America. It was stated that "We are here to win the war and not to spread bad propaganda about our country." The white soldiers, who were sitting on the side listening to the lecture, were upset with the officers for appealing to the colored soldiers. However, when Brazier's group reached India the white soldiers had already put their propaganda machine to work. They told the Indian women that all Negro soldiers had tails. Segregated USOs were established. Whites went to one and Negroes went to the other.

Enroute to India the ship stopped in Australia for about 3 days. Some of the soldiers, Brazier among

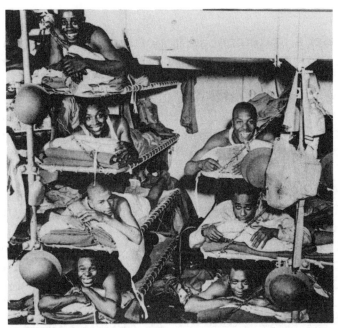

Black soldiers were stacked in the bottom of the troop ships like sardines.

them, were able to get off the ship. Brazier recalls that when he got off the ship and looked back at the rear deck he saw all Negro faces; the rest of the ship forward was all white. The view of the ship from the dock was a strong and vivid picture of the reality of Army segregation.

Staff Sergeant Brazier, #36386393 of the 1940s, is today Dr. Arthur M. Brazier, the pastor of the Apostoloic Church of God which has a membership of over 10,000 parishioners, and is located in the Woodlawn community of Chicago. When Dr. Brazier became pastor in 1960, the church had approximately 100 members. During the 34 years of his pastorate, he has led his congregation in two major remodeling programs and in the construction of two new church buildings, along with educational classrooms.

Following World War II in the decade of the fifties, when the Civil Rights Movement was gaining momentum, Dr. Brazier experienced a deep concern that Christian ministers become actively involved in the struggle for equal rights and justice. For Dr. Brazier it was a moment of decision. Many ministers of his denomination felt that the church had no role in the Civil Rights Movement, but Bishop Brazier disagreed.

Dr. Brazier coped well with the seemingly dichotomous position of a spiritual leader working within a movement that was concerned with achieving socio-economic goals. He realized that it was not the goal of the Civil Rights Movement to win souls for Christ. He did not try to change those goals, but instead tried to lend a spiritual input to the method of achieving them. It was from this perspective that Dr. Brazier became actively involved in the Civil Rights Movement and associated with one of the greatest leaders of our time, Dr. Martin Luther King Jr.

**U. S. DISTRICT JUDGE GEORGE NEVES LEIGHTON
FORMER INFANTRY CAPTAIN**

CHAPTER TWENTY-THREE

HE LEAPED FROM 7TH GRADE TO HOWARD UNIVERSITY AND HARVARD LAW SCHOOL

George Neves Leighton was born in New Bedford, Massachusetts on October 22, 1912. His father, Antonio N, and his mother, Anna Sylvia (Garcia), were people of very meager circumstance. They could ill afford to send both George and his twin sister Georgina to school in proper raiments or encourage him to stay; therefore, he dropped out of school in the 7th grade to perform a sundry of odd jobs around his small New England hometown.

Overriding the poverty that enveloped him was George's unquenchable thirst for book learning. His addiction to the library and its storage of knowledge was stronger than a junkie's craving for heroin. The big opportunity for him to display his love for the written word and his skills to use them came when the Seamans Memorial Fund, which was founded in honor of six Verdean Seaman who perished at sea, conducted an essay contest in the Spring of 1935. The top two winners would receive $200.00 each to pay tuition and expenses to go to the college of their choice. George, the 7th grade dropout, won one of the prizes and Henry R. Peters, a university junior, won the other.

George had written earlier to Mr. F. D. Wilkerson, the registrar at Howard University, expressing his strong desire and a legion of reasons for wanting to attend. In the registrar's reply dated September 3, 1935 he indicated that he had given careful consideration to George Leighton's request for admission and believed that his writing skills would enable him to do creditable work at the college level. However, the letter also stated that with no formal secondary training he would have to register as an unclassified student in the College of Liberal Arts. This, in substance, meant that George was on his own without the benefit of any assistance from the university. The post script in Mr. Wilkerson's letter further stated that if at a later date George decided to become a candidate for a degree he should be so advised.

In January 1936, George Leighton arrived on the Howard University campus in Washington, D. C. with the $200.00 scholarship money he had won and a small amount of additional currency he had saved from working as a dishwasher in restaurants and as a bell hop at hotels. The young, five feet, eleven inch, slender, copper-colored man from New Bedford, weighing slightly under 150 pounds, was a sight for sore eyes on the campus as he carried a small hand me down suitcase in which he had stuffed all of his worldly possessions, with the exception of the second hand suit he had on his back.

At the end of the first semester George N. Leighton searched out Mr. Wilkinson to show him that he had earned three As and two Bs in competition with upper middle-class Negroes from professional families. Mr. Wilkerson's reaction to the sight of Leighton's grades was to congratulate him and immediately advise his secretary to put George N. Leighton on the classified list of students working toward a degree.

In 1937, while working for his degree, George joined the Army Reserve Training Corps. He made the decision that if he ever fought in a war it was not going to be as an enlisted man. Joining the Army was a smart move because the smell of forthcoming World War II was permeating the air over the Pentagon. Germany invaded Poland in September 1939.

In January 1940 Leighton won another $200.00 prize in the New York Town Hall Essay Contest. His paper was second in a field of twelve thousand essayists. In mid-February 1940 Leighton began to suspect that he would be finishing near or at the top of his class. Believing that to be true, George went to Mr. William H. Hastie, Dean of the Howard Law School and a 1930 graduate of the Harvard Law School, and introduced himself. George requested Mr. Hastie's assistance in arranging a meeting for him to confer with the Dean of the Harvard Law School.

Three days after the meeting with Dean Hastie, George N. Leighton received a letter from James Landis McCauley, Dean of the Harvard Law School, inviting him to come to Cambridge. George journeyed by train to Cambridge and had a one-on-one talk with the Dean who invited him to come back to Harvard after he finished his undergraduate work at Howard in June 1940. George N. Leighton graduated second in his class, Magna Cum Laude; he was also inducted into the Phi Beta Kappa Honor Society.

Leighton was sailing smoothly through his studies at Harvard in the Fall of 1941 with the sons of the rich and the famous. The school was not admitting women in December 1941 when the Japanese bombed Pearl Harbor. In March 1942 his Army reserve commission became operative and he was ordered to report to the 369th Infantry at Fort Deven, Massachusetts on March 19, 1942. After taking a physical at Fort Deven, he proceeded to Fort Benning, Georgia where he was enrolled in the 206th Basic Class at the Infantry School on March 22, 1942. At Fort Benning he saw a

**Lieutenant George N. Leighton at
Fort Benning in March 1942.**

number of men he had known at Howard, including Edward Brooke, who later became a United States Senator from the State of Massachusetts. Lieutenant George N. Leighton completed his officers training at Fort Benning on June 17, 1942 and was immediately shipped to Fort Huachuca, Arizona to underdergo additional training in preparation for overseas duty with the 25th Infantry Service Unit of the 93rd Division. On January 31, 1944 the Division sailed from a port of debarkation near San Francisco, enroute to an unknown destination in the South Pacific. After 18 days on the water they arrived at Guadalcanal, in the Solomon Island, on February 18, 1944.

Captain George N. Leighton *(on left)* **on Guadalcanal in the Solomon Island in April 1944.**

Leighton served in the South Pacific for one year, eight months and eleven days. His tour of duty outside of the continental United States took him from Guadalcanal to Bougainville to Green Island, all of which are located within the Solomon chain of islands. It was in Green Island that the late Captain Charles Collins, a prominent Chicago mortician, was seriously wounded. Collins was not attached to the 25th Infantry Service, whose primary function was to mop up the Japanese stragglers in an area after the Marines and other combat units had routed the enemy.

Unlike the 25th Infantry Service Company the fighting 25th of the 92nd Division initially became responsible for the defense of the Finschhafen Port. The defense duty became minor when the need arose to retrain the colored riflemen and machine gunners for Quartermaster jobs such as winch operators, signalmen, and checkers. Those that were not retrained became common dock laborers. For four months, Negro fighting men unloaded ships.

By the time Leighton's service company reached Finschhafen, General Douglas McArthur was on his way back to Manila in the Philippines. George was promoted to Captain and assigned the responsibility of supervising the preparation and execution of logistical data for a regiment combat team (approximately 4,100 men).

In Morotai in the Dutch East Indies, Leighton became the Commanding Officer of the Japanese Detention Camp. One of his functions was to send patrols into the jungle to find the Japanese and hold them prisoners in a concentration camp. In October 1945, several months after the war had ended, Leighton was preoccupied with the thought of getting out of that dismal place and back into Harvard Law School.

Just like David, Leighton said: "I cried to the Lord and He Heard My Voice." The very next day the Army issued a directive that said that any person in the military service whose detainment would result in the loss of either an investment or a career, could write the Secretary of the Army and give the details. Leighton wrote a very persuasive letter but never got a response. Roughly a month after he wrote the letter the Army issued another directive stating that a person with so many points would be eligible to return to the states. George had the points based on months served but his return trip to Harvard made Homer's Odyssey seem like a very short journey.

After George graduated from Harvard Law School he was subsequently admitted to the Bar of the Commonwealth of Massachusetts on October 2, 1946.

His civilian career path after the war was as follows:

Partner in the law firm of Moore, Ming and Leighton, 1951-1959; McCoy, Ming and Leighton, 1959-1964; Judge of the Circuit Court of Cook County, 1964-1969; Appellate Court, 1st District of Northern Illinois, 1969-1976; U.S. District Judge, Northern District of Illinois, 1976-1986; of Council Earl Neal and Associates, 1987 to present.

CAPTAIN DAVID W. PELKEY

CHAPTER TWENTY-FOUR

THE HARD WORKING CAPTAIN WHO SELECTED NOT TO BECOME RICH

David W. Pelkey received his masters degree in political science from the University of Illinois at Champaign-Urbana in June 1940. His initial plan was to return to school in the Fall of 1940 and enroll in a two-year doctorate program. After a family meeting it was decided that he would volunteer for a one year hitch in the Army since he was a prime candidate for the draft. He had been classified as 1-A under the new Selective Service Act.

On November 6, 1940, Pelkey joined the 184th Field Artillery National Guard and was shipped to Fort Custer, Michigan on January 5, 1941 when the 184th was activated into active duty. Captain John Harris promoted Private Pelkey to Machine Gun Sergeant twenty-five days after the regiment reached Fort Custer on January 6.

In the Fall of 1940 the "top of the table" agenda being articulated by General George C. Marshall, U.S. Chief of Staff, was to give all National Guard Units one year of active service. However, subliminally everybody knew from the uncontrollable growling in their large gut that America was preparing to go to war. The officers and men of the 184th Regiment never made the upcoming war a part of any discussion. In August of 1941 the United States Chief of Staff extended the original twelve month active duty calendar for the National Guards to eighteen months. Four months later, on Sunday, December 7, 1941, the United States was attacked by Japanese Zeros diving out of the heavens, dropping bombs on both land and ships in the harbor of the island of Pearl Harbor, Hawaii. Active military service following this major disaster was automatically extended for the duration of the war plus six months.

The mind set of knowing that the Army was going to be your home for an indefinite period of time was not one to relish with glee unless you were a "jack in the box" career soldier. If you were not 4F (physically unfit) the option of not serving in the Armed Forces was to be absent without leave (AWOL), and ultimately going to prison. Fort Custer became a transient home for thousands of white and colored soldiers from both Michigan and Illinois. A relatively small percentage of new recruits went over the hill (AWOL) during the first twenty-four hours in the service.

Fort Custer had its colored neighborhood the same as Detroit, Michigan and Chicago, Illinois. The colored troops and officers were housed in a special pocket of the camp area, the same as they were in the cities. There was no escape from being colored, not even on paper. If a bulletin, general order, or special order was issued from the Service Command and a colored officer's name appeared on it, beside his name would be an asterisk, i.e. Major John Doe*. This was a code message to the white military world that you were not one of their kind.

Within the 184th Field Artillery you did not have to worry about being their kind to rise in the ranks because everybody was colored from the foot soldier to the colonel. Promotions were not based on race; your ability to perform was usually the barometer for moving up in rank. David Pelkey's performance was superior in that he was promoted from Sergeant to Second Lieutenant and Munitions Officer in the field while on maneuvers in Arkansas. His notice of the promotion was received in a telegram dated September 15, 1941

Captain Edward D. Wimp Jr. and his wife Elizabeth at 12th Street train station shortly before the Captain boarded the train for Camp Custer, Michigan on January 5, 1941.

to Lieutenant Colonel Marcus Ray, the Battalion Commander, from Colonel Anderson Pitts, the Regimental Commanding Officer.

An interesting side light to Pelkey's field promotion was that he had not been in the service twelve months and was not considered officer material by his immediate superior. Those who were anointed to be leaders in the 184th Field Artillery were given green bands to wear around the biceps of their left arms. Pelkey was serious, smart and low key. He was not a "lipstick wearer" or the kind of person who would make any effort to draw attention to himself.

For reasons unknown to David Pelkey he was never scheduled to take the Army's intelligence aptitude test, nor did he every apply or go to Officers Candidate School. He told the author, who has known him for over fifty years, that he thought that the reason he was considered for a field commission was because it was suspected by somebody on high that there was an outside possibility that he might have some sense. A year after he was made 2nd Lieutenant in the field he was promoted to 1st Lieutenant and Assistant Battery Executive under Captain E. Johnson. In November 1942 he became Commander of Headquarters Battery under Colonel Anderson Pitts.

In reference to his series of elevations David Pelkey said: "I worked hard on every assignment I was given. I would say that they did not give me anything but a chance. A chance for me was an opportunity to do the job. I was mentally and physically prepared to take advantage of the opportunity."

On January 17, 1943 the 184th Field Artillery was split up as a regiment at Fort Custer, Michigan. Some of the men were shipped to Camp Butner, North Carolina, under the command of Lieutenant Colonel Wendell T. Derrick of the 930th Field Artillery Battalion. David Pelkey and the other segment of the former regiment became the 931st Field Artillery under the command of Lieutenant Colonel Marcus Ray and were sent to Camp Forrest, Tennessee. It was in Tennessee that they were pulled out of the theater at gun point. (This incident is described by 1st Lieutenant Earl Strayhorn in detail in Chapter 20.)

Following the theater incident the 931st Field Artillery was sent to Camp Gordon, Georgia on April 28, 1943. It was in Camp Gordon that the enlisted men and all officers were separated. The enlisted men were sent to the Quartermasters and the officers were sent to the 92nd Division in Fort Huachuca, Arizona. The 92nd Division troops were colored and most of the officers were white, except for a handful of 2nd Lieutenants. The Negro officers from Camp Gordon replaced most of the white officers who were commanding colored troops.

Pelkey had been in command of a Field Artillery battery in Camp Custer, Michigan, Camp Forrest, Tennessee and Camp Gordon, Georgia. When he took over Battery A of the 600 Field Artillery Battalion at Fort Huachuca he used the same colored artillery officers that had been with him in the three aforementioned camps.

The men and officers of the 600 Field Artillery spent about one month getting their act together at Huachu-

(From left to right) Major General Almond, Commanding Officer of the 92nd Division, Colonel Marston, Executive Officer of the 92nd Infantry Division Artillery, Lieutenant Colonel Marcus Ray, Commanding Officer of the 600th Field Artillery Battalion, General George C. Marshall, Chief of Staff, U.S. Army, Brigidier General Coleburn, Commanding Officer of the 92nd Infantry Division Artillery and Captain David W. Pelkey, Commanding Officer Battery A, 600th Field Artillery Battalion at Fort Huachuca, Arizona on May 2, 1944.

ca before they headed for Camp Patrick Henry, Virginia, a port of embarkation, on April 14, 1944. When they reached the port in Virginia, Pelkey discovered that they had room on the ship for all the field artillery batteries except his. Like the late singer Otis Redding, he was left standing on the dock waiting for another ship to come in. Pelkey's Battery had to wait approximately a week before they were put on a ship. It was a French Luxury Liner converted into a troop steamer. Most of the troops on the ship were white Brazilians. This was the first time that Pelkey had witnessed white and colored Brazilians acting as if they were all the same complexion.

Since the ship was a luxury liner it was not part of a convoy like the ones that the 92nd Division had sailed on. Convoys move slowly. The convoy left a week before the luxury steamer arrived in Camp Patrick Henry, and yet Pelkey's Battery reached Italy a little better than a week before the other battalions arrived. Since Battery A had both men and guns they were put to work as a support group for the 10th Mountain Division. Battery A of the 600 Battalion had been under some heavy fire power before the other batteries arrived. Lieutenant Colonel Marcus Ray would stand around and watch the men and officers of Battery A until the shooting started. Then he would hastily remove his behind.

Captain David N. Pelkey describes an unusual combat situation: "During a tactically static development my Battery was put in a support position less than one half mile from the location separating the opposing ground troops. The position made it possible for us to

Captain David W. Pelkey's Champion Gun section of the 92nd Division crew of Battery A 600th Field Artillery Battalion goes into action in Italy.

effect interdiction and/or counter-battery fire four to five miles deep into hostile territory. At the same time, the nature of my equipment, 155mm howitzers, made the position tactically and logistically high-risk.

"To this, there was added a meaningful aggravating factor: Our troops occupied sea-level positions to the east of the mountains occupied by the opposing troops; those mountains gave unobstructed view of the entire area occupied by our troops. Certainly, it made it possible for observers in the mountains to see and locate a muzzle blast every time one of my guns was fired.

"Accordingly, for the first few days I was in that position, we fired missions only: 1) when directed by a liaison pilot in a 'put-put' and 2) when smoke generators effectively generated sufficient smoke cover in the area to preclude ready detection of muzzle blast.

"The day came when I was told that I had a fire mission without a smoke cover. That was, in my opinion, being told 'Pelkey, you are now a tactical sacrificial lamb'.

"I had, as standard operating procedure, effected reconnaissance for an alternate position; and while the gun sections were firing missions under 'put-put' direction we cleared the position of all the essential material and equipment.

"Although our muzzle blasts were clearly identified when we were firing without smoke cover, no retaliatory action was taken while the 'put-puts' were in the air; the pilots could have identified locations of counter-battery fire and directed our fire at those locations.

"As darkness approached, and the 'put-puts' left, we dug our guns out of position, loaded our ammunition and abandoned the position with a minimum of activity and delay.

"During that evening and night we could hear artillery fire landing in what I assumed was my recently abandoned position. Later, I went back; the area had been devastated by hostile fire."

The war ended in Europe in May 1945. Pelkey's Division stayed in Italy until November. Pelkey gives an eye witness account of how some soldiers got rich after the war ended.

"With no activity in Europe all the battalions were sent to the staging area to be sent back home or the Pacific except my battery. What they did with my battery, they sent us up to Geneva to take over security of the dock there. Why was that necessary? Because there had been this shipment of supplies, etc. These supplies and materials were enroute when the war ended. For example, ships still were coming in with field rations. The supplies had to be stored. Logistics dictated that supplies be piled up on the docks at Geneva and they had to have someone to guard them.

"So they took my battery. I was responsible for security at the docks. How much stuff was there? The 10 and 1 rations were piled up two stories high and a block long. If I had not been chicken I might have made some money or gone to jail.

"One day a man came to me and said 'we would like to use two of your trucks. Just let me have two trucks. I will give you $20,000 for each of the trucks.' He was saying he was going to load the trucks with supplies and take them and make some money. I am the guy who is in charge. All I had to do was say, take them and go, but I was chicken.

"I know one officer who was responsible for the Post Exchange merchandise. He sold two half ton trucks of PX supplies and reported that the trucks fell over one of those cliffs.

"Talking about making money. Guys would get MP arm bands. Just say three of them would get MP bands and one of them would take a jeep and catch a local citizen with some money and ask him if he wanted to buy a jeep. If the answer is positive you tell him to meet you on such and such a corner. The other two partners in this triangle of greed, wearing MP arm bands, would stop the guy on the next corner threaten to arrest him and take the jeep back. The three thieves end up with the jeep and the money. The number of soldiers who became rich in Europe will never be known."

After the war Pelkey graduated from law school and entered the private practice of law in Chicago, Illinois. Some years later he moved to Washington, D.C. and became an Administrative Judge for the General Services Administration where he conducted hearings and resolved disputes between government contracting personnel and firms having contracts to furnish supplies and services under contracts administered by such personnel.

In addition, he conducted hearings and resolved disputes as an Administrative Law Judge between Dept. of Labor contracting personnel and Dept. of Labor (DOL) contractors.

He also served as an Assistant General Counsel, Claims and Litigation Division, General Services Administration, where he supervised the activities of as many as 21 trial attorneys.

David W. Pelkey retired in February 1983. He still resides in Washington, D.C.

1st LIEUTENANT WELTON I. TAYLOR

CHAPTER TWENTY-FIVE

THE U OF I's FIRST IDENTIFIABLE NEGRO IN THE RESERVE OFFICER TRAINING CORPS

Welton I. Taylor graduated valedictorian in a class of 202 from Chicago's DuSable High School in June 1937, however, he did not give the class address. The president of the class, Jack Cosey, was given that honor because Taylor had only been a student at DuSable for one year whereas Cosey had been there four.

Taylor's Spanish teacher, Ms. Mercedes Rojas was livid because he did not get a scholarship, although eleven were given to members of his class. The eleven graduates who received the student aide had above average athletic ability in football, track, baseball and basketball. To comfort Taylor, Ms. Rojas said the following: "The last thing in the world a white man wants to see is an intelligent Negro man because he is competition. Those boys that they gave scholarships to are paid to run, jump and throw a ball. They are not competition to him in the real world. They are gladiators; paid gladiators."

Ms. Rojas, a shapely 5'2" teasingly beautiful brown skinned woman, was determined to see that Welton Taylor, a 6'2" gangling teen, went to college. She did not want to see this talented young man melt into the world of "should have beens". Through social contact she arranged for the studious Taylor to meet with some of the officers of Supreme Liberty Life Insurance Company, the largest Negro-owned life insurance company in the North. There she introduced him to Truman K. Gibson Sr., Earl B. Dickerson, W. Ellis Stewart, Jefferson G. Ish Jr. and several others. She told those men that they throw away more money playing poker on Saturday night than it would take to put this talented young man through college.

All the men at that meeting were members of the Kappa Alpha Psi Fraternity except T. K. Gibson Sr., who was an Alpha Phi Alpha. They agreed to give Taylor the assistance he needed. In addition, they told him he could live at the Kappa House in Champaign, Illinois and hopefully bring up the grade average because academically the house was in trouble. The boys were barely maintaining the 3.2 grade average needed to remain in good standing on the University of Illinois campus. Taylor's first-year 4.0 grade average lifted the house's average and the Kappa Alpha Psi Fraternity gave him a scholarship every year thereafter until he graduated in June 1941.

Taylor, a light-complexioned Negro, maintains that he was the first identifiable colored student to get a commission in the University of Illinois' Advance Reserve Officer Training Program. Edward D. Wimp Jr., a white-complexioned Negro, had finished the same program eight years earlier. Since I knew both of them it does not matter who was first. Both of them were intellectually sharp and subsequently became excellent Army officers in World War II.

The vanilla ice cream complexioned Welton Taylor created a problem for Major "Snuffy" Cole, a West Pointer and Professor of Military Science and Tactics at the University of Illinois. One morning at a breakfast from which Taylor was excluded the following dialogue took place. Major Cole said: "You all know Welton Taylor, the fellow that wears the corporal outfit at your drills?" The group responded with mumbles and positive nods of heads.

Captain Edward D. Wimp Jr.

Major Cole continued: "You know we go to summer camp every year for six weeks up at Camp McCoy, Wisconsin. We sleep four men to a tent. That means that the colored fellow is going to have to sleep with three of you guys. The Army cannot be in the position of having a separate tent for him to sleep in and a separate place for him to eat three meals a day. Therefore you have to vote now to determine whether we are going to accept him on the terms of everybody else or reject him. If we accept him he will sleep in whatever tent his name indicates, going alphabetically." A cadet named Harry Gruesome raised his hand and said: "He can sleep in my tent because he smells a damn sight better than most of you guys."

A number of cadets shared Harry's sentiment and one yelled, "Taylor is alright." Over in a corner there was a sorehead from Cairo, Illinois who said: "I don't want him in my tent."

Several men responded like a choir: "We don't want you in our tent." Major Cole said: "It seems like he is in." The response from the group was: "Yeah!" Early that afternoon Major Cole called Taylor to his office and said: "Get fitted for your uniform, your boots, brown belt and hat. I will be looking for you at 11:00 o'clock drill tomorrow, Cadet Lieutenant Welton Taylor."

Twenty eight days after Taylor graduated from the University of Illinois in June 1941, he was on a train enroute to Fort Sills, Oklahoma. He was in the company of a group of white officers from Illinois and Michigan. When the train passed through Missouri the conductor tapped Taylor on the shoulder and said, "You are going to have to move up front to the colored car". Taylor gave the conductor a short course on interstate law and the conductor told him he would have an opportunity to explain the law to the Sheriff in the next town if he did not move out of that seat in 15 minutes. Taylor tucked his tail, bowed his head, picked up his bag and headed for the colored car. He found coal dust all over the place, the windows were open, and the noise from the steam engine was deafening. He closed his window in an effort to keep the coal dust off of his uniform.

His first assignment at Fort Sills was with a training battalion. The commanding officer classified himself as a blue blood from Boston, Back Bay Bostonian. He was a tall gaunt 6'5" alcoholic. His uniforms were tailored from the finest material. His second in command in the battalion was a white First Lieutenant who was transferred shortly after Taylor arrived. That move caused Taylor to move up in responsibility without an elevation in rank. The Captain did not run the outfit; he dropped that duty into Taylor's lap. The Captain's nightly hangovers would not permit him to make reveille. Taylor took reveille and reported to the Captain after lunch because when the Captain got out of bed each morning, he headed straight for the Officer's Club to get a morning eye opener. Technically the Officer's Club was not supposed to open until 4:00 pm. It was never open to Negroes.

Taylor was constantly on the phone calling the Captain at the Club in an effort to get solutions to the daily problems that crossed his desk. Sometimes, if the Captain was sloppy drunk, he would tell Taylor, in a slurred voice, to use his own judgement.

Officer's mess had open seating for everybody except Negroes. Since there were only two colored officers on the Post, Chaplain Oscar Holder, a Major from Baltimore, Maryland, and Taylor, the mess officer made special arrangements for them. He set up a table for two. The Mess Sergeant in charge was a big 250 pound colored fellow from Oakland, California, with a voice that had the volume of a bull horn. At meal time the officers, North and South, would line up for chow. The line was always at least a New York City block long. They fed over one thousand officers in rotation at each meal. The Mess Sergeant always stood at the door to make sure nobody crashed the line. However, when he saw Major Holder and Lieutenant Taylor walking across the horizon down that hot dusty road he would holler out without restraint in his bull horn voice, "Major Holder and Lieutenant Taylor your table is ready!" His action really got the attention of the Colonel, Lieutenant Colonels, and Majors standing in that blazing Oklahoma sun waiting for their meals. The sergeant poured salt on the wound when he put a fresh rose in a vase in the middle of Holder's and Taylor's table every day. Off the record the Sergeant said: "If they are going to segregate you officers I am going to rub their nose in it. Enjoy."

The "tea for two" days ended like they started. Suddenly. Taylor was assigned to the 93rd, which was on red alert with orders to go overseas. The 93rd Division was an all-Negro outfit up to Colonel.

First Lieutenant Welton I. Taylor recalls the following sequence of events prior to going overseas. He completed Field Artillery Battery Officers School in August 1942 after 12 weeks. In June 1943 he entered the Army Air Force Basic Flying School which he completed in August 1943 after 8 weeks. The training was followed by a Field Artillery Liaison Pilot Training School for six weeks and completed in October 1943.

Taylor saw seven fatal crashes in seven weeks, each a student and an instructor--14 people! By graduation time there were several other Negro pilot-trainees still in the course. Sam Evans failed and was sent home and First Lieutenant Jones hit a white First Lieutenant who used the word "niggers" in his presence, and was washed out in check flights the next day.

On January 31, 1944 the 93rd Division left Camp Stovenaw, California and set sail for "somewhere in the

Pacific". The ship was the Willard A. Holbrook (President Taft cruise ship). Two enemy submarines picked them up just outside of the San Francisco Bay and trailed them for three days before it was out-distanced at 23 knots! Two weeks later the Holbrook picked up a destroyer escort near New Caledonia and proceeded to the harbor of Talagi. That night while Taylor was watching the lightening flashes and listening to the thunder on the horizon, he was informed by a ships' officer that what looked like a storm was actually Japanese and American warships in a fire-fight off the shores of Guadalcanal--where they were to land at 0800 hours the next day! That turned out to be the

Army Air Force Liaison Training Detachment at Pittsburg, Kansas. The only colored pilot officer is 1st Lieutenant Welton I. Taylor, *(top row left)* **Flight Leader 2nd Squadron (fourth highest ranking officer in the unit).** *(Third from the right in front row)* **is 2nd Lieutenant "Van" Van de Kamp of the food-seafood chain.**

last such fight on Guadalcanal because U.S. supremacy became established throughout the Solomon Islands.

Taylor did not experience any combat duties on Guadalcanal. However, he saw five of their artillery men
killed when a shell exploded while being loaded into a
155mm howitzer. As a temporary Safety Officer Taylor
had photographed the gun and crew just prior to the
explosion and had been blown into a ravine by the
blast. An hour earlier he had witnessed a mid-air col-
lision between a P-38 and P-39 "dogfighting". The faster, less maneuverable '38 had dropped flaps to tighten
his turn to prevent the slower '39 from turning inside
and getting his tail. This maneuver caused the '39 to
sever the twin tail bone of the '38 sending both planes
plunging into the sea. While two parachutes opened
and both were picked up almost instantly by a destroyer in the bay, one pilot was dead with a broken neck.
Wars have occupational hazards, not enemy initiated,
too.

Taylor's duties as an Air Observation Pilot included
piloting a single engine aircraft assigned to the 93rd
Division and being responsible to the commander for
performing missions involving aerial observation. He
flew reconnaissance missions to locate enemy units
and installations, and spot camouflage areas and activities. In advances against, and by the enemy, he located and directed fields of fire, located routes of ap-
proach, and observed and estimated strength, type of
enemy units, and their deployment. In addition he reported findings and received orders while in flight, by
radio.

After the war Taylor married Jayne Kemp of Morgan Park in 1945 and they returned to the University of Illinois under the GI Bill for advanced degrees. He obtained his M.S. in 1947 and Ph.D. in 1948, the first time such an accelerated program had ever been permitted. He returned to Chicago and became an instructor in microbiology in the University of Illinois School of Medicine. He has also invented and patented a line of microbiological diagnostic kits for laboratory use and has opened a manufacturing laboratory to make his devices.

He is a Diplomate of the American Board of Medical Microbiologists, a Fellow of the Academy of Microbiolo-

This colored and white outhouse was not in Georgia it was in Guadalcanal.

gy, and an Associate Professor of Microbiology at the University of Illinois Medical Center.

In 1985, in recognition of 35 years of research into food poisoning, the Centers for Disease Control (CDC) named a new species of bacteria in his honor, Enterobactertaybrae. This was the first such honor for an African American scientist.

University of Illinois diploma.

Appendix B

STATEMENT BY RONALD V. DELLUMS, CHAIRMAN OF THE HOUSE ARMED SERVICES COMMITTEE

"I am deeply troubled by the findings of the report {of the House Armed Services Committee Task Force on Equality of Treatment and Opportunity in the Armed Services} which indicate to me that far too many of our men and women in uniform believe that their careers are jeopardized by acts of discrimination and prejudice in the services. When we fail to pay attention to such a basic and crucial issue as equal opportunity, the message communicated to our service members around the globe is that we do not equally value each person's potential to make a contribution. This is a dangerous and delerious situation that must be addressed, both because of its improper negative impact on individual careers and its overall impact on the morale and readiness of the force.

"Fortunately, there are steps that can be taken, indeed they must be taken, to create a positive equal opportunity climate. As the report notes, the commitment of leadership to equal opportunity is the primary determinant of the racial climate at a facility. The significance of this finding is clear: It is imperative that support come from the DoD and service leadership - at all levels. There must be a consistent, and, where necessary, a renewed leadership commitment to accept the responsibility to construct a working environment in which each and every officer and enlisted person will be treated with dignity and accorded respect.

"I look forward to working with the incoming majority as we continue to address these important issues during the 104th Congress."

Appendix C

HOUSE ARMED SERVICES COMMITTEE STAFF TASK FORCE ON EQUALITY OF TREATMENT AND OPPORTUNITY IN THE ARMED SERVICES

"AN ASSESSMENT OF RACIAL DISCRIMINATION IN THE MILITARY: A GLOBAL PERSPECTIVE"

DECEMBER 30, 1994

I. Introduction

In response to a rise in the number of discrimination complaints received by the House Armed Services Committee, along with other indicators of potential problems of racial and ethnic discrimination in the armed services, the Chairman of the Committee appointed a bi-partisan staff task force in November 1993 to assess the nature and scope of discrimination as it exists in the services today. This report summarizes the findings of the Task Force based upon its work over the past twelve months, including interviews with approximately 2,000 service members at 19 military facilities in the United States, Europe and Asia.

II. Summary of Findings

The Task Force's findings comprise a complex web of good news and bad news. Of the nineteen military installations visited by Task Force teams, only one of those installations evidenced an extremely elevated level of racial tension, and a profound range of negative equal opportunity indicators. In contrast, at most of the facilities assessed by the Task Force, racial tensions were relatively muted, and while problems of race discrimination were evident to varying degrees at every facility, many service members rated the equal opportunity climate at their facilities positive.

Overt forms of racism, including racial slurs, racial jokes and racist graffiti, were reported as commonplace at four of the nineteen facilities visited by the Task Force, and were reported at lower levels at some of the other facilities. Wide differences in perceptions between majority and minority members existed at many facilities, both as to the frequency of such behaviors and the extent to which such behaviors were deemed acceptable, accepted or tolerated. It is worth noting that white supremacy and skinhead activity by service members was reported at several facilities; at one facility, both majority and minority members reported that it occurs at a level that poses a threat to good order. However, many service members reported that overt forms of racism were not tolerated within their units, and leadership response to such conduct is swift and appropriate.

These overt forms of racism, however, placed a distant second in terms of prevalence. The predominant and most damaging forms of discrimination reported by service members at most facilities involve subtle forms of racism that, nonetheless, have significant adverse impact on minorities, particularly in the areas of career advancement and disciplinary actions.

Although the scope of discrimination has produced levels of racial tension that appear to be well under the "boiling point," the frequency with which similar themes were sounded, relating to grievance systems, disciplinary actions, career progression, access to mentoring, equal opportunity training, and cross-cultural understanding, point to the need for the Department of Defense and the individual services to improve their equal opportunity efforts. A failure to do so could lead to elevated tension, and will in any event, diminish the capability and readiness of the force.

As a general rule, senior members reported less discrimination and a better EO climate, while junior members reported more discrimination and lack of trust in the complaint system. Majority enlisted personnel, and to some extent majority junior officers, frequently perceived instances of reverse discrimination and expressed resentment at efforts by minorities to demonstrate or exhibit aspects of minority culture or separatism.

At virtually every facility, minority members expressed their concern that the minority community tended to incur disproportionate discipline, both in frequency and severity. Because the services early reports to the Task Force indicated that records maintained by each of the services reflect disparities in discipline based on race, we believe this issue warrants much further exploration.

Although at every installation equal opportunity complaints were being investigated and resolved, and some senior members at some facilities believed that the formal complain system worked well, significant problems with the complaint system were pervasively reported. At virtually every facility, the task force repeatedly heard that:

- The lodging of a complaint carried with it a substantial risk of retaliation.

- The risk of retaliation discouraged many from using the system, even when an individual had the support of his or her own immediate chain of command and the weight of evidence supported the person lodging the complaint.

- In situations where service policies or regulations rigidly prescribed the chain of command as the exclusive channel for lodging and resolving complaints, service members were more likely to perceive the possibility of or experience actual retribution for filing a complaint.

Other areas of concern regularly reported to the Task Force include lack of training relating to race or ethnicity concerns, cultural ignorance, and the stereotyping of minorities. It was very commonly reported that virtually all recent EO training received by service members relates to sexual harassment, with many reporting that they have received no or very little training on racial issues. Others reported that the training they received was ineffective, consisting of little more than a slide presentation by a poorly trained individual. The lack of effective training was underscored by the fact that racial stereotypes and lack of cross-cultural understanding cropped up frequently in Task Force interview sessions. It is notable that in many interview sessions conducted by the task Force, service members expressed a strong interest in having small group interactive training sessions similar to the Task Force interview sessions. Although these interview sessions were not intended to be educational sessions, they did appear to serve an educational function for many participants because they encouraged frank discussion of real-life racial issues in a confidential, small-group setting.

Minorities frequently reported the perception that "doing your job to the best of your ability" was not a guarantor of promotion, good assignments, or other career enhancing actions. In addition, minorities also perceived they had to conform to the predominantly majority social and institutional norms of the military society in general, and their particular unit or work group specifically -- to become "one of the good old boys" -- in other words, to get favorable consideration. The truth of these perceptions appeared to be validated to some extent by majority members who commented negatively on innocuous cultural expressions that were identified with minorities, including such seemingly trivial issues as music choice, hairstyle, off-duty dress, and choice of leisure activities.

Minorities generally felt that the "good old boy" systems favored majority members, in part because of low minority representation in particular specialties, commands, and senior leadership. Mentoring was reported as one means to help minorities break the effects of subtle discrimination inherent in the military society; yet, many more majority members than minority members reported that mentoring was available to them.

Perhaps the most significant, and ultimately hopeful, finding of the Task Force is the fact that a commitment of leadership to equal opportunity is the primary determinant of the racial climate at a facility. Only two of the nineteen facilities visited by the Task Force had leadership that appeared indifferent (or, in one case, hostile) to equal opportunity issues. But commitment of leadership encompasses much more, of course, than saying the right thing, and service members are quick to perceive the sincerity and depth of commitment from their leaders. Where leadership was viewed by service members as paying only "lip service" to equal opportunity issues, or where leadership perceived race relations as a problem that "had been licked in the 70's and 80's", racial problems and tensions appeared to be greater, and a wider gulf existed between minority and majority perspectives. Where leadership viewed the effort of providing and maintaining equal opportunity for all as requiring a daily, constant, multifaceted effort, the overall climate of the installation appeared positive (particularly where that leadership had significant tenure).

An important caveat with respect to the impact of top leadership should be noted. The Task Force found, at some facilities, that even deeply committed leadership lacked knowledge of race discrimination issues at their facilities because information was blocked from rising up the chain of command. This appears to occur at times because some junior officers and senior NCOs fear that the presence of a racial problem in their unit will reflect on their leadership; at other times, it appears to occur because the drive to solve problems at the lowest level means that there is a great reluctance to allow problems to surface up the chain of command, even if they are not adequately addressed or addressable at lower levels. A critical aspect of strong top leadership, therefore, is developing mechanisms to ensure that critical information rises through "middle management" to the top.

BIBLIOGRAPHY

INTERVIEWS
Black, Corporal Timuel D., 8/30/94, 9/30/94, 8/30/94
Brazier, Staff Sergeant Arthur, 11/15/94
Campbell, Staff Sergeant Wendell, 9/9/94
Coleman, Seaman 1st Class David C., 8/9/94
Cousins, 1st Lieutenant William, 3/15/91
Deas, 1st Lieutenant Milton B., 9/9/94, 1/2/95, 9/9/94
Gardner, Sergeant Edward G., 9/6/94
Gardner, Staff Sergeant Frank, 8/23/94
Gibson, Civilian Aide Truman K. Jr. ,7/6/94, 12/4/94, 7/6/94
Hervey, 1st Lieutenant Henry P.,8/26/94
Johnson, Judge E.C., 8/29/94
Jones, Third Class Petty Officer Mark, 9/30/94
Kirkpatrick, Captain Felix, 8/29/94, 8/29/94, 9/2/94, 9/29/94,
Leighton, Captain George N., 9/22/94, 1/23/95
Long, Staff Sergeant Alvin C., 9/12/94
Martin, Captain Robert, 9/8/94
Myles, Corporal Eddie, 8/20/94, 10/10/94
Pelkey, Captain David, 1/9/95, 1/12/95
Rogers, Captain John W., 9/1/94, 11/27/94
Russell, Ensign Harvey, 9/25/94
Skinner, Corporal Clementine, 9/29/94
Stewart, Private Wilborn, 8/25/94
Strayhorn, Lieutenant Earl, 8/22/94, 1/9/95
Taylor, 1st Lieutenant George, 9/1/94,
Taylor, Corporal Raymond, 5/30/94, 8/30/95, 9/30/94
Taylor, 1st Lieutenant Welton, 2/20/95, 2/22/95, 10/4/94, 9/27/94
Thatcher, Lieutenant Colonel Harold W., 9/29/94, 10/13/94
Thomas, 1st Sergeant Joseph, 8/19/94
Thompson, 1st Lieutenant Bill, 9/1/94
Washington, 1st Sergeant Harold, 4/23/83, 4/31/83, 5/31/83,
    1/2/84, 8/16/84, 5/12/84, 5/19/84, 7/14/84, 4/18/85, 8/12/85,
    10/15/86, 9/22/86, 10/18/86
Westbrook, 1st Lieutenant Shelby, 9/14/94
Wheeler, Sergeant Lloyd , 9/6/94, 12/19/94, 12/21/94
Williams, 1st Lieutenant James B., 4/28/90, 12/7/94, 12/19/94

BOOKS
*A Historical and Pictorial View of the National Guard and Naval
    Militia of the State of Illinois*, Army and Navy Publishing
    Company Inc., Baton Rouge, Louisiana, 1940.
Adams, Russell L., *Great Negroes: Past and Present*,
    Afro-Am Publishing Company, Chicago, 1963.
Allen, Robert A. L., *Chicago Fort Mutiny*, Armistead, New York, 1993.

Aptheker, Herbert, *The Negro People in the United States 1933-1945*, Citadel Press, Secaucus, New Jersey, 1974.

Bailey, Beth and Farber, David, *The First Strange Place :The Alchemy of Race and Sex in World War II Hawaii*, The Free Press, New York City, 1992.

Davis, Benjamin O. Jr., *Benjamin O. Davis Jr. America: An Autobiography*, A. Pluma Books, New York City, 1992.

Duis, Perry R. and LaFrance, Scott, *We Have A Job To Do: Chicagoans In World War II*, Chicago Histrical Society, 1992.

Early, Charity Adams, *One Woman's Army: A Black Officer Remembers The WAC*, Texas A & M University Press, Carlonstation, Texas, 1989.

Edelman, Bernard, *Dear America: Letters From Home From Vietnam*, Pocket Books, New York, London and Toronto, 1985.

Editors of Ebony, Introduction by Lerone Bennett Jr., *Ebony Pictorial History of Black America*, Johnson Publishing Company, Inc., Chicago, 1971.

Editors of Ebony Magazine, Ebony Suceess Library Volume I, *1,000 Successful Blacks*, Johnson Publication Company, Inc. Chicago, 1973.

Editors of Time-Life Books, *This Fabulous Century: Sixty Years of American Life, Vol. III*, 1969.

Greene, Ewell Robert, *Black Defenders of America, 1975-1973*, Johnson Publishing Company, Inc., Chicago, 1974.

Groupman, Alan L., *The Air Force Integrates, 1945-1964*, the Office of Air Force History, United States Air Force, Washington, D.C., 1985.

Killens, John Oliver, *And Then We Heard The Thunder*, Albert A. North, New York City, 1963.

Lee, Erwin, H., *Negro Medal Of Honor Men*, Dart, Mead & Company, New York, 1969.

Lee, Ulysses, *The United States Army in World War II Special Studies: The Employment of Negro Troops* Washington D.C. Office of the Chief of Military History the United States Army, 1966.

MacGregor, Morris J. Jr., *Integration of Armed Forces, 1940-1965*, 1985.

MacGregor, Morris, J. and Nalty, Berna, *Black In The United States Armed Forces: Basic Documents Vol. V*, Scholarly Resource, Wilmington, Delaware, 1977.

Morris, Herman C. and Henderson, Harry B., *World War II In Pictures, Volume II*, The Journal of Living Publishing Corporation, New York, 1945.

Motley, Mary Penick, *"The Invisible Soldier"*, Wayne State University Press, Detroit, 1975.

Nalty, Bernard, *Strength for the Fight, A History of Black Americans In The Military*, The Free Press, New York, 1986.

Parks, Gordon *Voices In The Mirror: An Autobiography*, Doubleday, New York City, 1990.

Philips, J. Alfred, *Chappie: America's First Four Star General The Life and Times of Daniel James Jr.*, Presidio, 1991.

Potter, Lou, Miles, William and Rosenblum, Nina, *Liberators: Fighting On Two Fronts In World War II*, Hartcourt Brace, New York, 1992.

Robinson, Jackie, *I Never Had It Made, As Told To Alfred Duckett*, J. P. Putnam's Sons, New York, 1972.

Rowan, Carl T., *Breaking Barriers: A Memoir*, Little Brown & Company, Boston, Toronto and London, 1991.

Rust, Art, Jr., Edna and Louis, Joe, *Joe Louis: My Life*, Hartcourt Brace Jovanovich, New York and London, 1978.

Stillwell, Paul, *The Golden Thirteen : Recollections of the First Black Naval Officers*, Naval Institute Press, Annapolis, Maryland, 1993.

Sulzberger, C. L., *The American Heritage Picture History of WWII*, The American Heritage Publishing Company, New York City, 1966.

Terkel, Studs, *The Good War*, Pantheon Books, New York City, 1984.

The Negro In Chicago: A Study of Race Relations and A Race Riot in 1919, Arno Press and New York Times, New York, 1968.

Travis, Dempsey J., *An Autobiography of Black Politics*, Urban Research Press, Chicago, 1987.

Travis, Dempsey, J., *I Refuse To Learn To Fail*, Urban Research Press, Chicago, 1992.

Travis, Dempsey J., *Harold The Peoples Mayor,*, Urban Research Press Inc. , Chicago, 1989.

Travis, Dempsey J., *The Autobiography of Black Chicago*, Urban Research Press Inc., Chicago, 1981.

Tuttle, William A. Jr., *A People and A Nation: A History of the United States*, University of Kansas et al, Houghman, Lipman Company, Boston, 1982.

Waters, Enoch P., *American Diary*, Path Press Inc., Chicago, 1987.

Westbrook, Shelbey,*Tuskegee Airmen: 1941-1945*, Tuskegee Airmen Inc., Chicago Chapter, 1992.

NEWSPAPER ARTICLES

"Stimson's Removal Is Demanded By Dawson", Chicago Defender, March 4, 1940.

"Army Rushes Plans For All-Negro Division; Issues Call For Volunteers", Chicago Defender, December 20, 1941.

"Abe Lincoln Ordered Acceptance of Negroes Into All U.S. Armed Forces", Chicago Defender, December 27, 1941.

"Nine Soldiers Go Hungry 22 Hours On Train Only Because of ' Color'", Chicago Defender, May 16, 1942.

"Chicago Boys Tell Of Army Riot In Louisiana", Chicago Defender, January 17, 1942.

"Chicago Soldiers Flee South During New Reign Of Terror", Chicago Defender, September 1942.

"The Truth About Belgium's Congo and World War II", Afro-American, August 22, 1942.

"Graduation of WAAC's Set for 29th", Afro-American, August 22, 1942.

"L.A. Soldiers Found Guilty of Attack", Afro-American, August 15, 1942.
"1st Group of WAAC Graduates Will Be Sent to Ft. Huachuca",
    Afro-American, August 15, 1942.
"Willkie Says He'd End Navy Jim Crow", Afro-American, April 4, 1942.
""White Man's War" Treason Case Is All Washed Up",
    Afro-American, March 6, 1942.
"10 U-Boat Survivors Save Whites But Get Jim-Crowed at Port",
    Afro-American, June 27, 1942.
"New York Official Lauds Our Soldiers In Plea for Unity",
    Afro-American, June 27, 1942.
"Navy Training Head Is Trustee of Hampton Inst.", Afro-American,
    June 27, 1942.
"Afro Sends War Department Letter from Soldier at Sea",
    Afro-American, November 7, 1942.
"17 Crack Line Officers at Aberdeen", Afro-American, October 28, 1942.
"Soldiers from Eleven States Assigned to Camp Swift"
    Afro-American, October 28, 1942.
"93rd Artillery Units End Mock Warfare", Afro-American, October 31, 1942.
"Rankin Gives Notice Colored People Will Be "Kept in Their Place,"
    War or No War", Afro-American, April 4, 1942.
"Army Paper Tells Interesting Story of Tank-Driving Men", Afro-American,
    December 12, 1942.
"150 to Get CAA Pilot Training", Afro-American, September 12, 1942.
"Ollie Stewart's First Cable from Britain", Afro-American, Sept. 12, 1942.
"I Got Wings: First Colored Flyer Tells His Story", Aro-American,
    July 18, 1942.
"How A Man Gets His Wings At Tuskegee", Afro-American, Oct. 24, 1942.
"Brigadier General B.O. Davis Sr. in Phoenix Investigating the Riot",
    Afro-American, December 5, 1942.
"Lieutenant Is Slugged in Indiana Cafe", Afro-American, Dec. 5, 1942.
"What the Daily Press Thinks of the New Jim-Crow Navy Rules",
    Afro-American, April 8, 1942.
"Jim Crow Draft Call" Afro-American, December 5, 1942.
"Army Nurse Beaten by Cops In Ala.", Afro-American, Sept. 26, 1942.
"FBI Accuses 80 in Chicago of Part in Seditious Activities",
    Afro-American, September 26,1942.
"Chaplains Tell Soldiers to Wait for Girls Back Home",
    Afro-American, July 18, 1942.
"Divinite Arrested for Ignorin Draft; Says He's Only Six",
    Afro-American, July 18, 1942.
"Drive On For 100 WAC Recruits By November 7", Afro-American,
    October 16, 1943.
"Says WAAC Is No Refuge for Frustrated Females", Afro-American,
    June 5, 1943.
"Chicago Woman Passes Tests, Becomes A WAAC",
    Afro-American, February 6, 1943.
"Order Halts Recruit Drive For Race WAACs", Afro-American,
    June 19, 1943.

"Navy Cross Won By Third Negro For Rescuing Mate",
   Afro-American, June 19, 1943.
*"Romance Takes Back Seat Among WAAC's; All Love Strictly Bound By
   Rank In Army"*, Chicago Defender, January 23, 1943.
*"Segregation Rules WAAC Training Camp; Race Volunteers Lag Far
   Behind Quota"*, Chicago Defender, January 16, 1943.
"Negro Crews To Man Anti-Submarine Vessels", Chicago Defender,
   February 26, 1943.
"Navy Quota For Draftees Boosted To 15% For Race", 'Chicago Defender,
May 8, 1943.
"Court Martial Imposes Harsh Punishment In Tennessee Camp"
   Chicago Defender, December 4, 1943.
"64 Soldiers Jailes For Use of Army Trucks", Chicago Defender,
   December 4, 1943.
"War Or No War, East Alton Keeps Its No-Negro Habits", Chicago Defender,
   February 3, 1945.
"Ship Held Two Days Because Captain Balked at Officers",
   Afro-American, July 24, 1943.
"No Democracy for Sailors Shipwrecked", Afro-American, July 24, 1943.
"Drive J.C. from the Army", Afro-American, July 24, 1943.
"To Name Liberty Ship for Robert S. Abbott", Chicago Defender,
   March 11, 1943.
"Troops Resent Stimson's Slur, On Ability Of Negro Combat Units",
   Chicago Defender, March 11, 1943.
"Chicagoans Face Enemy Fire On Anzio Beachhead", Chicago Defender,
   March 11, 1943.
"Three Soldiers to Hang", Afro-American, August 14, 1948.
"Tain Held an Hour to Jim Crow Officer", Afro-American, June 5, 1943.
"General Stockton Reminds Soldiers They Were Slaves",
   Afro-American, August 14, 1943.
"Colonel Pitts and Staff of 7 Lose Command", Chicago Defender,
   Jaury 23, 1943.
*"Is Jim Crow Ban In Army Possible? Civil War A Lesson For
   Today*, Chicago Defender, March 20, 1943.
"Navy Boss Knox Bars Mixed Crws In Navy", Chicago Defender,
   November 20, 1943.
"White Soldier Fined For Dancing With Negro Girl", Chicago Defender,
   November 27, 1943.
"Confederate Flag For Dixie Troops, Senator Proposes", Chicago Defender,
   November 27, 1943.
"Hit Jim Crow Navy Badges", Chicago Defender, November 27, 1943.
"Soldier Gets 25 Years In Coast Racial Outbreak", Chicago Defender,
   August 28, 1943.
"Chicago Men In Armed Service", Chicago Defender, October 9, 1943.
"Sgt. Deas Promoted to Lieutenant", Chicago Defender, February 6, 943.
"Guilty of Draft Evasion", Chicago Defender, February 6, 1943.
"Why I Resigned! by William H. Hastie", Chicago Defender, Feb. 6, 1943.

"Judge Advocate Mccoy Is Promoted To Major" Chicago Defender,
 November 4, 1943.
"Tuskegee Aaces", Chicago Tribune, July 25, 1991.
"Easter 1943 Lost To War Torn World", Chicago Defender, April 24, 1943.
"Whites protest Negroes at Michigan Army Air Base", Chicago Defender,
 April 24, 1943.
"War Workers Take Wives to Hawaii", Afro-American,
 March 27, 1943.
"Rickenbacker Favors Jim Crow Air Force", Afro-American,
 March 27, 1943.
*"Hastie Tells How Negro Air Heroes Get Run-Around By Army
 Brasshats"*, Chicago Defender, February 13, 1943.
"Tuskegee Pilots Now At Big Michigan Air Field", Chicago Defender,
 April 10, 1943.
"99th Ready To Leave for Combat", chicago Defender, February 20, 1943.
"S. S. Booker T. Brings Muni tions To North Africa" Chicago Defender,
 April 24, 1943.
"Segregated Air Base Planned In N. Africa", Chicago Defender,
 June 18, 1943.
"Congress Told No Negro Combat Troops At Fronts", Chicago Defender,
 November 6, 1943.
"First Navigation Cadets Arrive At Texas Air Base", Chicago Defender,
 November 6, 1943.
"Gibson Named To Replace Judge Hastie", Chicago Defender,
 February 13, 1943.
"South Whipping Negro Soldiers Report Says", Chicago Defender,
 April 29, 1944.
"Film Corp. Tries To Halt Showing of 'Negro Soldier'", Chicago Defender,
 April 29, 1944.
"Man Guns In Battle Against Axis Army", Chicago Defender, June 10,1944
"DuSable Grad In Charge of U.S. Air Force Station", Chicago Defender,
 June 10, 1944
"Scores Jim-Crow Tactics At Fifth War Loan Dinner" , Chicago Defender,
 June 10, 1944.
"12 Nazi Planes Shot Down By 99th Pursuit Squadron", Chicago Defender,
 February 5, 1944.
"Details Of Hawaii Mutiny Told By Defender Scribe", Chicago Defender,
 February 17, 1945.
"73 GI's Convicted For Hawaii Mutiny", Chicago Defender, Feb. 3, 1945.
"Chicago Clergyman Gives 6 Sons to War, Loses Five", Chicago Defemder,
 February 3, 1945.
"Two More Congressmen Support Mixed Army", Chicago Defender,
 January 5, 1946.
"Clear Officer In Loading Of Negro Troops", Chicago Defender,
 January 5, 1946.
"General Bradley Okays Jim Crow Rule In Dixie", Chicago Defender,
 January 12, 1946.

"GI Killed By White Sentry, Manila Troops Start Riot", Chicago Defender,
    January 12, 1946.
"World War II's Black Pilots Fought On Two Fronts", New York Times,
    April 21, 1991.
"Navy's First Female Combat Pilot Loses Sea Duty", New York Times,
    January 23, 1995.
"Black Sailors Recognized for World War II Heroism", New York Times,
    February 14, 1995.
"Comrades and Family Fighting to Honor a Hero", New York Times,
    March 28, 1993.
"Vietnam Troops Considered To Stop King", Chicago Defender,
    March 29, 1993.

MAGAZINES

"Black Violators of the Draft", Common Sense Magazine, December 1942.
"Winfred Lynn Case Again: Segregation in the Armed Forces",
    The Social Service Review Magazine, December 1944.
"Let's Look At The Record", Common Sense Magazine, October 1944.
"The Draft", American History Magazine, October 1994.
"The G.I. Bill May Be the Best Deal Ever Made by Uncle Sam",
    Smihsonian Magazine, June 1994.
""Journal of Negro Life", Opportunity Magazine, January-March 1945.
"The Brownsville Incident", Ebony Magazine, March 1973.
The Good War", Chicago Tribne Magazine, December 1, 1991.
"We've Come A Long Way. . .", Forbes Magazine, September 14, 1992.
"Tuskegee Airmen, Still Flying High", Ebony Magazine, November 1994.
"Crossing the Lines on Silent Wings", Smithsonian Magazine, June 1994.

JOURNALS & PAMPHLETS

"The Negro and World War II", Negro Handbook, 1944.
"Some Mutinies, Riots, and Other Disturbances", Negro Handbook,1946-47
"The Negro Policy of the American Army Since World War II",
    Journal of Negro History, April 1953.
"Roosevelt, Foraker, and the Brownsville Affray", Journal of Negro
    History, January 1956.
"Lawlessness and Violence In America", Journal of Negro History,
    January 1959.
"The Impact of the Second World War on the American Negro",
    Journal of Contemporary History, 1971.
"What The Negro Soldier Thinks About This War",
    Journal of Contemporary History, 1972.
"Judge Hastie, World War II, and Army Racism", Journal of Negro History,
    October 1977.
*"Conspiracy to Discredit the Black Buffaloes: The 92nd Infantry in
    World War II"*, Journal of Negro History, Winter/Spring 1987.
"Their War and Mine", The Journal of American History, September 1990.
"History of Blacks in the Coast Guard From 1790", Department of Transp.

INDEX